The Christmas Stocking

★ The Pat Richards Crafts Collection ★

The Christmas Stocking

Elegant Projects for the Holidays

Photography by Bill Milne

FRIEDMAN/FAIRFAX
PUBLISHERS

A FRIEDMAN/FAIRFAX BOOK

Library of Congress Cataloging-in-Publication data available upon request.

ISBN 1-56799-369-9

Editor: Francine Hornberger
Art Director: Lynne Yeamans
Designers: Joseph Rutt and Andrea Karman
Photography Director: Christopher C. Bain
Photography by Bill Milne/New York

Color separations by Bright Arts Graphics (S) Pte Ltd.
Printed in the United Kingdom by Butler and Tanner, Ltd.

Every effort has been made to present the information in this book in a clear, complete,
and accurate manner. It is important that all instructions be clearly understood before
beginning a project. Please follow instructions carefully. Due to the variability of materials
and skills, end results may vary. The publisher and the author expressly disclaim any and
all liability resulting from injuries, damages, or other losses incurred as a result of material
presented herein. The author also suggests refraining from using glass, beads,
or buttons on stockings intended for small children.

For bulk purchases and special sales, please contact:
Friedman/Fairfax Publishers
Attention: Sales Department
15 West 26th Street
New York, New York 10010
212/685-6610   FAX 212/685-1307

Visit the Friedman/Fairfax Website:
http://www.webcom.com/friedman

I'd like to dedicate this book to Mark, Keith, and Lee

for their patience, support, and understanding, and without

whom Christmas would be just another day.

Thanks to Amy Syrell for her help in preparing these stockings.

Contents

≈≈≈≈≈≈

≈≈≈≈≈≈

Introduction

When I was a child, Christmas stockings played a huge part in our family Christmas celebrations. Before I was born, or at least long before I can remember, my grandmother gave my mother a number of heavy old-fashioned stockings and orphaned hunting socks to be turned into Christmas stockings. My mother embroidered our names on them with red and green yarn, adding a few decorative motifs and silver jingle bells to complete the effect.

The empty stockings would go up during the holiday decorating of the house and hang there temptingly, in anticipation of Santa's visit and what he would leave us. From then on we would spend long hours in our rooms, mapping out the location of the squeaky boards in our floors so they could be avoided on Christmas Eve. We were not supposed to touch those stockings until a "reasonable" hour on Christmas morning, but the thought of the unknown treats in those now bulging stockings was just too much temptation for us, and we tiptoed down the stairs long before we were allowed. We were never bold enough to actually take anything from our stockings before the prescribed time—just spying on the contents and trying to figure out what was hidden deep inside was excitement enough. How our parents failed to hear us I will never know—perhaps they did. But they knew it was all part of the fun. As you can conclude from the joy my humble hunting sock stocking gave me, a stocking doesn't have to be an elaborate or expensive work of art. But if you enjoy creating beautiful things, making a special stocking is a simple, manageable, and thoroughly gratifying project. A Christmas stocking made with your own hands makes a delightful gift for anyone.

When I had my first child, I wanted to make a stocking for him that would be special and would bring as much joy to him in our holiday celebrations as those very plain and unassuming stockings had brought for me. I selected a beautiful cross-stitch pattern of polar bears and added a ribbon and candy-cane border of my own design to integrate the arrangement with the stocking body, and finished it by adding his name across the cuff. A few years later my second son arrived. The stocking I created for him evolved into a wonderful hand-embroidered, crazy-quilt pattern, and has embodied for him all that same joy and holiday magic.

The stockings shown here are designed as much to inspire you as they are items for you to re-create. Each design was inspired by materials found in the fabric and notion stores around me and from the visual impressions I gathered in my travels through life. Study them, re-create them if you wish, or look around you at what materials are available, think about what techniques you might like to explore, and let these stockings serve as the launching pad for your own talents and imagination.

Each of the four basic patterns on which these stockings are based was designed to the same scale and requires a ½-yard (45.5cm) length of fabric for the stocking itself and/or the lining. Obviously the patterns will not use up the entire ½ yard (45.5cm). You may therefore wish to go through your scrap basket to see if you have something suitable, especially for the lining, before going out to purchase additional fabric. When shopping for stocking fabric, keep your mind open—you may find your ideas changing and evolving with the materials you encounter.

You will find that some of these stockings are lined, and some are not. If the stocking fabric was relatively lightweight, or especially drapable, I lined it so it would hold its shape better when hanging. Heavier-weight fabrics that could hold up on their own were left unlined. If the stocking will be functional, you may wish to line the stocking simply to finish off the inside neatly. It is your decision.

The hanger, too, is a place where the options are endless. Most of my stockings hang from a piece of the fabric from which they are made. That is an easy option. The width and length of the hanger can be altered at your whim or you can create a fancy bow and hanger from ribbon.

Stockings you make for yourself or someone you love have a very personal significance. Even if you simply create your masterpiece from a variety of materials already at your disposal, the fact that you took the time and love to create something unique is an incredible gift that the recipient will cherish for years to come.

Chapter One
~ ~ ~ ~ ~ ~
Fun & Folksy

There is an old saying that simplicity is its own reward. If that is so, then the stockings featured here have their place guaranteed forever in our hearts, as their design is based upon the most simple of stocking shapes. This is the shape a child might make when asked to draw a stocking.

This stocking shape's uncomplicated lines recall frontier holidays when Christmas was celebrated with that which was at hand. A stocking at that time would probably have been your largest and most hole-free sock (you wouldn't want any treasures to fall out!). When people moved on to fashioning more permanent holiday decorations, stockings were created from the scraps of a beloved old quilt or pieced from remnants of Dad's plaid workshirts—as are two of the examples you'll find among the designs in this chapter.

The simple shape of these stockings does not mean they should be limited to a "country" look, as you'll see in the variation made from laminated Sunday comics and the caveman version, laced up in fake fur with a couple of hanging clay "bones."

General stocking pattern for chapter
Enlarge to 172%

Country Plaid Stocking

An assortment of plaids in

holiday colors lends a country casual feel to

this patchwork stocking which bears a pieced pine

tree motif on its center front diamond.

MATERIALS

½ yd (45.5cm) of red-and-brown plaid fabric

Scraps of 5 plaid fabrics, including at least one predominantly green plaid

Scraps of beige-and-black striped and light beige marbled fabrics

Small piece of brown fabric

½ yd (45.5cm) of brown fabric for lining (optional; you will have enough from the red-and-brown plaid to line the stocking as well)

Sewing thread

Enlarge stocking pattern (page 11) and inset diamond pattern (page 14), adding ¼" (6mm) seam allowance to all pieces and ½" (1.5cm) to top edges of stocking and cuff. For the insert diamond, cut tree pieces from green plaid, background pieces from beige marbled fabric, trunk from brown, and borders from beige-and-black striped fabric. Cut stocking front pieces from assorted plaids. Cut stocking back and four cuff pieces from red-and-brown plaid. Cut stocking lining from brown.

Assemble tree square first, sewing pieces into rows and then sewing rows to make a square. Sew border strips to each side of square,

mitering corners to finish diamond inset. Sew each stocking front piece to the diamond first, then to adjacent stocking piece. With right sides together, sew assembled stocking front to stocking back using a ¼" (6mm) seam. Clip curves and turn right side out. Press. Sew stocking lining pieces together using a ⅜" (1cm) seam. Trim seam allowance to ⅛" (3mm) and slip inside pieced stocking. Align top edges and baste together.

Sew side seams of each set of cuff pieces. With right sides together, sew cuff lining to cuff along bottom edge and turn right side out. Press. With right side of cuff facing wrong side of stocking, align top edges and stitch together using a ¼" (6mm) seam. With machine set on zigzag, stitch over raw edges of cuff and stocking tops. Turn cuff to outside. For hanger, cut a 2" × 7½" (5 × 19cm) strip from any of the plaid fabrics. With right sides together, fold in half lengthwise and stitch long edge with a ¼" (6mm) seam. Turn right side out and press flat. Fold in half, and tucking under raw ends, stitch in place to inside back edge of stocking top.

≈ VARIATIONS ≈

You might want to try a different motif in the center medallion of this stocking—a stocking, star, mitten, or snowman, or maybe even an initial. The motif doesn't have to be pieced: appliqué it, embroider it, or even paint it. The stocking itself need not be pieced either. Make it of a single plaid fabric, plaid flannel, or even a solid.

Diamond inset pattern
Shown at 100%

Paper Dolls Stocking

Inspired by the paper-doll chains we all made as youngsters, this stocking with its bright red and green appliqués makes a perfect graphic accent to your holiday decorations.

MATERIALS

½ yd (45.5cm) unbleached muslin

¼ yd (23cm) each green and red prints

Red and green rayon embroidery threads to match

½ yd (45.5cm) lightweight paper backed fusible adhesive

Enlarge and trace appliqué patterns (page 16) to paper backing of fusible adhesive adding ¼" (6mm) seam allowances to edges of appliqués. Following manufacturer's directions, fuse trees to back of green fabric, and all other pieces to red. Cut out on marked lines.

Using stocking pattern (page 11), cut two with ¼" (6mm) seam allowance all around and two with slightly less than ¼" (6mm) seam allowance. Following pattern, fuse appliqués to front and back stocking pieces. With machine set on medium satin stitch and threaded on top with matching rayon thread, satin stitch along all cut edges of appliqués. With right sides together, stitch stocking front to back, using a ¼" (6mm) seam. Clip curves and turn right side out. Using a ¼" (6mm) seam, stitch lining pieces together and slip inside stocking. Pin raw edges together around top.

From remaining green fabric, cut a strip 1⅛" × 16" (3 × 40.5) for binding. Fold under ¼" (6mm) at beginning of strip and with

Appliqué Pattern
1 square = 1 inch
Enlarge to 203%

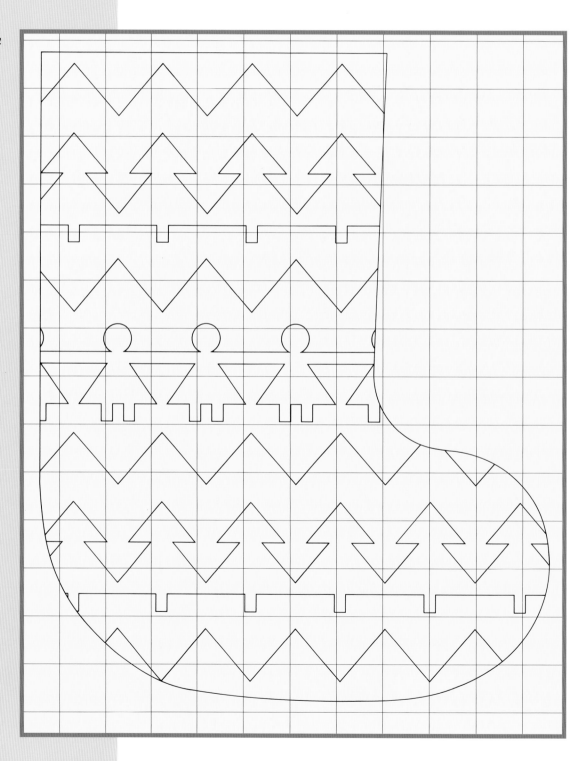

right sides together and raw edges even, sew to top edge of stocking and lining using a ¼" (6mm) seam. Fold binding to inside of stocking, turning under raw edges and slipstitch folded edge over seam line. Cut another strip from green 1¼" × 9" (3 × 23cm) for hanger. Fold strip in half lengthwise, folding raw edges to center. Slipstitch folded edges together. Fold strip in half and stitch ends to top inside edge of stocking.

~ VARIATIONS ~

The stark red and green fabrics work well for this stocking, but the use of different colors or a more casual fabric would look charming as well. Substitute little boy paper dolls for the girls, or add an image that's significant to your life—perhaps a new house or car.

Comic Strip Stocking

Favorite comic strips, a child's drawing,

or beautiful gift wrap paper can be easily turned

into a functional or purely decorative stocking.

MATERIALS

Colored newspaper comic pages

1 yd (91.5cm) each of Heatn'Bond Iron-On Flexible Vinyl and Heatn'Bond Ultra Hold paper-backed fusible adhesive

Lightweight paper

3 yds (5.5m) of black cord

Hole punch

White craft glue

Enlarge stocking pattern (page 11), adding ¾" (2cm) hem allowance at top edge only. Select comic strips you want to use on the front, and piece them together to make an area slightly larger than stocking pattern. If necessary, lightly tape pieces together in front. Do the same for stocking back. Following manufacturer's directions, fuse adhesive to back of assembled stocking pieces. Fuse these pieces to lightweight paper. Apply iron-on vinyl to right side of front and back assembled stocking pieces. Trace stocking pattern onto each piece and cut out. Fold ¾" (2cm) hem allowance to inside along top edge and glue in place. With wrong sides together, lightly tape both pieces together and mark for lacing holes, ⅛" (3cm) inside of edge and ⅝" (1.5cm) apart. Using hole punch, make holes where marked. Leaving approximately 12" (30.5cm) of cord at top back edge, lace through holes all around. Knot cord at top front edge and trim excess. At upper back edge, form a 3½" (9cm) loop with remaining cord and knot at base of loop. Reinforce knots with glue.

∼ VARIATIONS ∼

Any printed paper, whether from a newspaper or magazine, wrapping paper, or even a child's piece of artwork can be used to make this whimsical stocking. Smaller paper pieces may be joined to form a sheet large enough from which to cut the front of the stocking. Simply tape pieces together lightly on the front, trim overlapping edges to approximately ¼" (6mm) and fuse to backing paper. Finish as described in the instructions for this stocking.

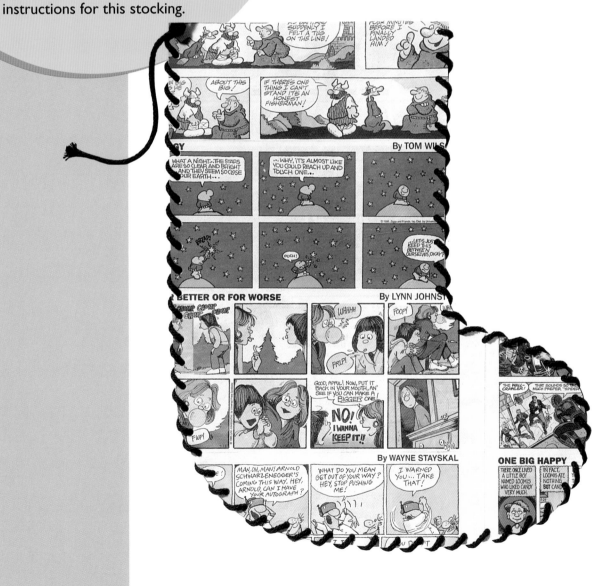

Pennsylvania Dutch Appliquéd Stocking

Graphic depictions of a bird, tree,

and heart, symbols commonly found in

Pennsylvania Dutch art, combine with the technique

of buttonhole appliqué to make a stocking rich

in simple elegance.

Enlarge stocking pattern (page 11), adding ¼" (6mm) seam allowance all around. Cut two stocking pieces from off-white fabric. With machine set on medium-width zigzag, stitch around all edges of stocking front. Trace motif shapes (page 22) onto paper backing of fusible adhesive. Following manufacturer's directions, fuse shapes to appropriate color fabrics. Cut out appliqués (page 22), position on stocking front as shown, and fuse in place. With three strands of embroidery floss, work blanket stitching around all exposed edges of appliqués. With right sides together, sew stocking front to back using

MATERIALS

½ yd (45.5cm) of "homespun"-looking, off-white fabric

¼ yd (23cm) of red cotton fabric

Small pieces of red, two shades of purple, and three shades of green fabrics

¼ yd (23cm) of paper-backed fusible adhesive

1 skein of dark brown-black embroidery floss

Sewing thread

¼" (6mm) seam. Clip curves and turn right side out, pressing seams flat. Cut a 3½" × 17" (9 × 43cm) strip of red fabric. Wrap around top of stocking and mark seam line. With right sides together, sew cuff side seam; trim excess fabric. With right sides together and top edges even, stitch cuff to stocking with a ¼" (6mm) seam. Press seam allowances toward cuff. With embroidery floss, work blanket stitching along seam. Fold cuff self-lining to inside, turning under ¼" (6mm) on raw edge. Slipstitch folded edge to cuff seam line on inside of stocking. For hanger, cut a 2½" × 8" (6.5 × 20.5cm) strip of red fabric. With right sides together, fold in half lengthwise and stitch ¼" (6mm) from long raw edge. Turn right side out, fold in half, and sew securely to inside back edge, tucking raw ends under.

toe piece

Appliqué patterns
1 square = 1 inch
Enlarge to 207%

Southwestern Style Stocking

Silver conchos laced onto

black leather trim the cuff of this

stocking sewn from colorful serape-type fabric

for a festive but casual look.

MATERIALS

½ yd (45.5cm) of colorful striped fabric

4 silver conchos

½ yd (45.5cm) of leather lacing, ¼"
(6mm) wide

1 yd (91.5cm) of leather cord

2 silver cord tips

Craft glue

Fabric glue (optional)

Sewing thread

Enlarge stocking pattern (page 11) and cuff pattern (page 25), adding ¼" (6mm) seam allowance all around stocking and cuff, adding ¾" (2cm) hem allowance to bottom of cuff. Cut two each of stocking and cuff from striped fabric. With right sides together, sew side seams of cuff and sides and bottom of stocking using ¼" (6mm) seams. Clip curves and turn both right side out. Fold under ¾" (2cm) hem allowance of cuff and fabric-glue or sew in

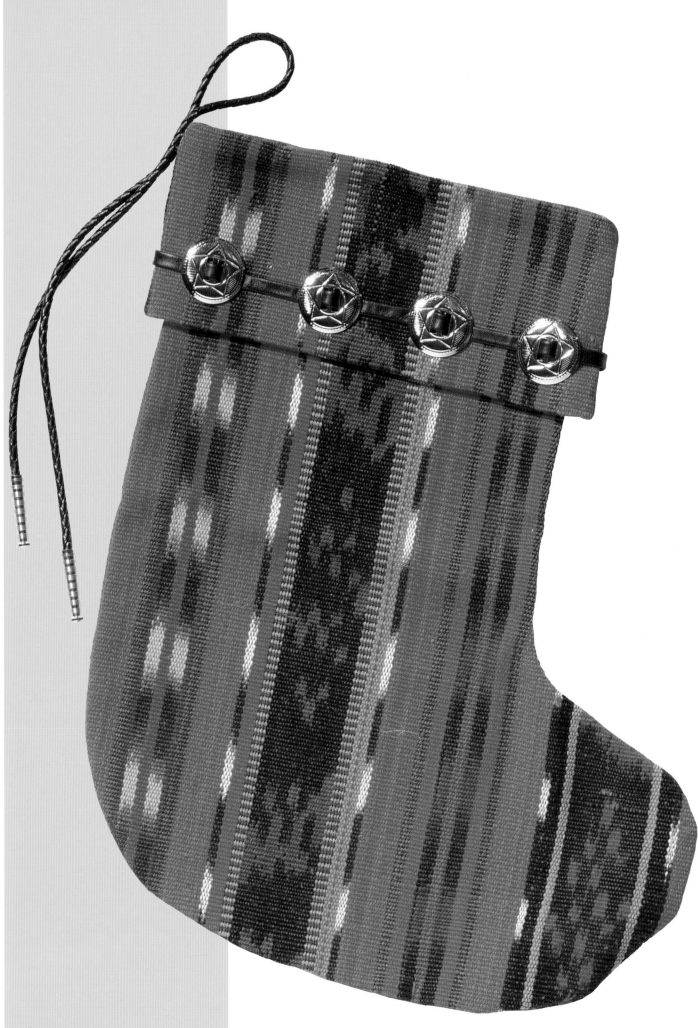

place. With right side of cuff facing wrong side of stocking, pin cuff inside stocking aligning side seams and top edges. Sew stocking to cuff using ¼" (6mm) seam. Turn cuff to outside. Thread conchos onto leather lacing and position on front of cuff. Fabric-glue or sew in place. For hanger, fold leather cord in half and tack to back edge of stocking top. Trim ends to desired length and glue tips to ends of cord with craft glue.

Cuff

Pattern shown at 100%

Pinwheel Patchwork Stocking

Whether created from a scrap

of an old family quilt, or from patterns provided

here, this casual stocking trimmed with buttons

will lend a warm touch to your holiday festivities.

1 yd (91.5cm) of white cotton fabric

Assorted scraps of printed cotton fabrics

½ yd (45.5cm) of lightweight batting

Assorted white and mother-of-pearl buttons

Twine

Sewing thread

Trace patchwork patterns (page 28) to cardboard or template plastic adding ¼" (6mm) seam allowance to triangles and cut out an equal number of print and white triangles. You will need approximately 30 pieced squares, necessitating 120 each of white and print triangles. Cut out approximately 26 white squares. Sew print pairs of and white triangles together along long sides using a ¼" (6mm) seam to form squares. Open and press seams to one side. Sew four squares together to make a larger square, having print triangles form pinwheel pattern. Sew pieced squares alternately with white squares to form a strip, then sew strips together to form a piece of patchwork large enough

Because this stocking is composed of square blocks, any basic quilting book can provide a number of other patterns from which to construct it. Size the pattern, via your neighborhood copy shop, to make a 3" to 4" (7.5 to 10cm) square, and assemble the squares according to the same directions. You might also consider tea-dying the quilted piece—to produce an older look—before cutting out the stocking. Embellishments are limited only by your imagination. Charms might look really cute, or consider adding a cuff.

(approximately 24" [61cm] square) to cut out front and back of stocking with squares set on point as shown in photograph. Make sure you have allowed excess all around, as pieced fabric may shrink when washed. Lay remaining white fabric right side down on flat surface. Smooth batting over backing. Center pieced fabric right side up on batting. Baste or pin layers together. Machine quilt along seam lines of large squares. If desired, wash quilted piece at this point to give it a worn look, or tea-dye it for an antique appearance.

Enlarge stocking pattern, adding ½" (1.5cm) seam allowance to sides and bottom and 1" (2.5cm) seam allowance to top. Cut stocking front and back from quilted piece. With right sides together, sew sides and bottom using a ⅜" (1cm) seam. Zigzag around top edge of stocking. Clip curves and turn right side out. Fold top edge to inside and slipstitch in place. Arrange buttons along top edge of stocking and sew in place. For hanger, cut three 9" (23cm) lengths of twine. Holding all three pieces together, knot the middle and tack ends to inside back edge of stocking top.

Patchwork patterns
1 square = 1 inch
Enlarge to 200%

All Buttoned Up Stocking

A multitude of buttons in a variety of sizes helps to transform an ordinary red-and-white striped dish towel into a cheery stocking with a casual country feel.

MATERIALS

Red-and-white striped dish towel

½ yd (45.5cm) of lining fabric

½ yd (45.5cm) of fusible interfacing

2 yds (1.8m) of narrow red piping

Assorted buttons (I used 21 green, 9 white, 18 red, and 1 yellow star; they range in size from ½" to 1⅛" [1.5cm to 3cm] in diameter, it pays to buy a few extra to play with)

Matching threads

Removable plastic adhesive

Note: One dish towel may not be large enough to cut two identical pieces for front and back. On mine the stripes run vertically on front, horizontally on the back. If this bothers you, purchase a second dish towel.

Enlarge stocking pattern (page 11). Trace twice to fusible interfacing, flopping pattern to create front and back pieces. Cut out, adding approximately ½" (1.5cm) all around. Fuse pieces to back of dish towel and cut stocking front and back from fused areas of dish towel adding a ¼" (6mm) seam allowance all around. From lining fabric cut two stocking pieces adding ¼" (6mm) seam allowance all around.

Pin piping to stocking front along seam line of sides and bottom. Sew along seam line having stitching just at base of piping and raw edges of piping within seam allowance. Pin stocking front to back, right sides together and sew along, or just inside, piping stitching.

Clip curves and turn right side out, pressing seams flat. Arrange buttons on stocking front and mark position or use plastic adhesive to hold them in place for stitching. Using matching threads, stitch buttons in place, removing all trace of plastic adhesive as you go.

Stitch lining pieces together along sides and bottom using a ¼" (6mm) seam. Pin piping around top edge and stitch in place, same as for stocking front and overlapping ends at back side edge. Slip lining over stocking (right sides together) and pin top edges together having raw edges even. Stitch along front and just past side seams, using a ¼" (6mm) seam, leaving remainder of back seam open for turning. Turn lining to inside of stocking and fold in raw edges of opening. Slipstitch folded edge of stocking to stitching line of piping. For hanger, cut a strip of towel 1¾" × 7" (4.5 × 18cm). Fold long edges under ¼" (6mm) twice and topstitch in place close to fold. Fold hanger in half and stitch ends in place to inside back edge of stocking top.

≈ VARIATIONS ≈

This stocking evolved because of the buttons I found around me. If your tree is made entirely from small, fairly uniform green buttons, you could try decorating it with some unique buttons, like gingerbread men or candy canes, or even plain balls or small stars. If you can't locate a good supply of green you could create a red-and-white-button candy cane, a gingerbread man with brown buttons, or a snowman from white buttons.

Caveman Stocking

Here is a humorous stocking crafted of fake fur and sporting two "bones" made from oven-hardening clay. It will provoke a smile from all who see it hanging on your mantel.

MATERIALS

½ yd (45.5cm) of jaguar print fake fur fabric

5" × 17" (13 × 43cm) piece of curly black fake fur fabric

3 yds (2.7m) of black leather lacing

Black sewing thread

Small sharp scissors

White polymer clay (oven bake type)

Glue (optional)

Enlarge stocking pattern (page 11), adding ¼" (6mm) seam allowance all around. Cut two stocking pieces from jaguar print. With right sides together, stitch around sides and bottom using a ¼" (6mm) seam. Clip curves and turn right side out. Beginning at one side seam, about 1" (2.5cm) from top edge, use a pair of small-bladed sharp scissors to poke a hole through both layers of fabric about ¼" (6mm) inside of edge. Working with a 2-yard (1.8m) length of lacing, tie a knot near one end and thread through hole just made. Continue poking holes at 1" (2.5cm) intervals and threading lacing through. If necessary, wrap a bit of tape around end of lacing to make threading it through the holes easier. End lacing about 1" (2.5cm) from top on opposite side of stocking. Knot lacing and trim excess. If desired, reinforce knots with glue.

Wrap black fur strip around top of stocking and mark side seam line. Stitch seam and trim any excess fabric. With right side of black fur facing wrong side of jaguar fur and edges even, stitch cuff to stocking top. Fold cuff to right side, turn under a ¾" (2cm) hem along raw edge, and slipstitch in place.

From white clay, form two "bones," each approximately 2½" (6.5cm) long. Bake following manufacturer's directions. Form remaining lacing into two 4" (10cm) loops with ends hanging about 8" (20.5cm) beyond that. Stitch base of loops to outside back edge of stocking. When bones have cooled, tie one to each end of lacing. Reinforce knots with glue, if desired.

Chapter Two
~ ~ ~ ~ ~
# Cool & Contemporary

Still a clean and simple shape, this chapter's stockings are based on a pattern in which the toe slopes down at an angle from the leg, thereby softening the right-angled look of the pattern in chapter one. This second pattern lends a more modern, geometric look, one that is reminiscent of the mod or pop stylings of the sixties and seventies when design was streamlined.

Here you'll find stockings with a crisp urban feel: a tailored menswear stocking in grey wool and a black felt model with shimmering gold and silver stars. I've warmed up the shape a bit by creating a stocking abloom with holly leaves and decorated with "berries," and sweetened another with favorite holiday candies and cookies.

General stocking pattern for chapter
Enlarge to 145%

Holly and Berries Stocking

Simply shaped holly leaves in bold

Christmas greens contrasting with bright

red-wooden-bead berries turn an ordinary stocking

into a Christmas treasure.

MATERIALS

½ yd (45.5cm) of white felt

1 square each of 3 shades of green felt

*22 red wooden beads, approximately
⁷⁄₁₆" (1cm) in diameter*

*1 skein each of red and green
embroidery floss*

*1½ yds (1.4m) of red velvet ribbon,
1½" (4cm) wide*

Red and white sewing threads

nlarge stocking pattern (page 35), adding ¼" (6mm) seam allowance on all sides and 1" (2.5cm) hem allowance at top. Cut two stocking pieces from white felt. Stitch a ¼" (6mm) seam around sides and bottom. Trim seam allowances around curves and turn right side out. Fold hem allowance to inside and sew in place.

Using both leaf patterns (page 38), cut several from each color of felt. Beginning at the toe, place several leaves in varying directions to cover white background as completely as desired. Pin leaves in place. Thread needle with three strands of green floss, and use a large straight

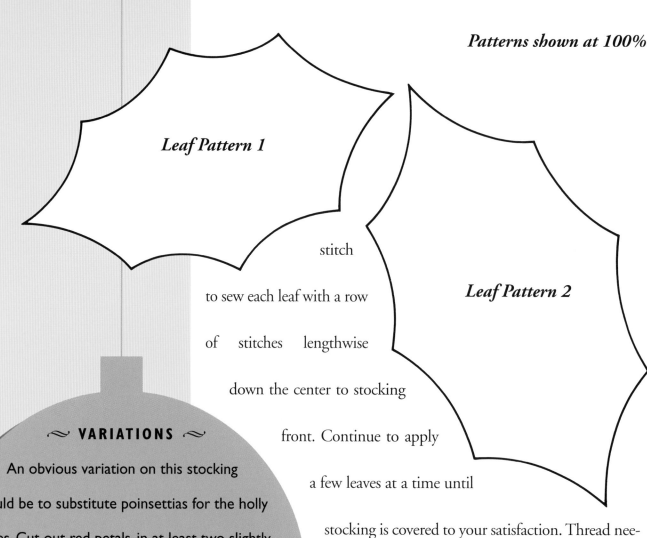

Leaf Pattern 1

Leaf Pattern 2

stitch to sew each leaf with a row of stitches lengthwise down the center to stocking front. Continue to apply a few leaves at a time until stocking is covered to your satisfaction. Thread needle with three strands of red floss and stitch beads to leaves at random locations over stocking front.

For hanger, fold ribbon in half and use red thread to gather both widths of ribbon tightly about 4" (10cm) below fold. Do not cut ribbon. To make bow, use remaining ribbon to make loops, gathering and tacking them to base of hanging loop. When satisfied with bow's appearance, tack to back edge of stocking top. Trim ends to desired length.

∾ VARIATIONS ∾

An obvious variation on this stocking would be to substitute poinsettias for the holly leaves. Cut out red petals, in at least two slightly different sizes and from at least two shades of red, and stitch them to the stocking, down the center of each petal, as for the holly leaves. Add a few leaves behind and between the flowers, and cluster several yellow beads in the center of each flower.

Ultrasuede Lace-Up

The bold splash of color made by this sexy, shocking pink Ultrasuede stocking will brighten the holiday greens draped across your mantel!

MATERIALS:

½ yd (45.5cm) of hot pink Ultrasuede

26 silver-tone eyelets and installing tool (you might want to purchase extras with which to practice)

Matching thread

Rubber cement

Tape

3 yds (2.7m) ball chain or silver cord

28 gauge craft wire

Note: It is difficult to pin into Ultrasuede. I transferred pattern markings by tracing them with a pencil on the wrong side, then went over them on the right side to transfer them to the Ultrasuede. Hold pieces together for sewing with tape (or use double-stick tape) between the two pieces near the seam line.

Enlarge stocking patterns (page 40). Cut one of each front piece along outside lines. Seam allowances are included.

Using general pattern (page 35), cut one back piece adding ¼" (6mm) seam allowance around sides and bottom, 1" (2.5cm) across top edge.

On wrong side of all pieces, apply rubber cement to stocking top seam allowance and to corresponding area on stocking body. Fold seam allowance to inside and weight with book or other flat heavy object until dry.

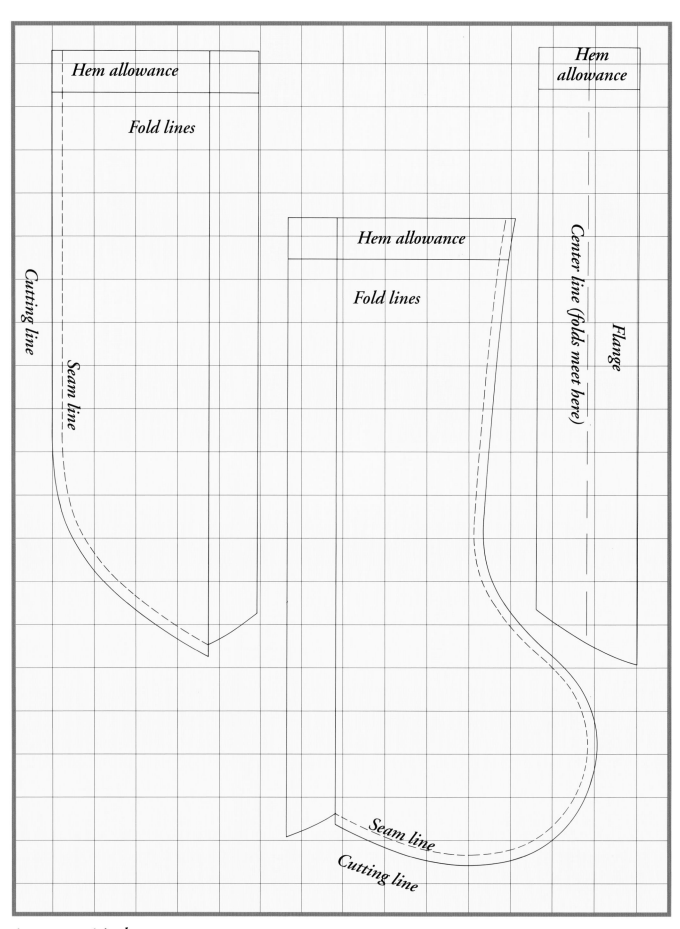

Hem allowance

Fold lines

Hem allowance

Fold lines

Hem allowance

Cutting line

Seam line

Center line (folds meet here)

Flange

Seam line

Cutting line

1 square = 1 inch
Enlarge patterns to 225%

With right sides together, and using tape to hold edges in place, align top and sides of flange with inner sides of front pieces and stitch from top to bottom edge using a ¼" (6mm) seam. Fold front pieces back on themselves along fold lines, taking care that folds meet in center of flange and completely cover it. Apply rubber cement to back of fold area on both front pieces. Fold along fold lines and weight with heavy book until dry. Beginning ½" (1.5cm) from top edge and ⅝" (1.5cm) from fold, mark each fold at 1" (2.5cm) intervals for eyelet placement. Using tool, punch holes at marks and install eyelets. It is a very good idea to practice installing eyelets on scraps of Ultrasuede before working on the stocking itself.

When all eyelets have been installed, place front and back right sides together, securing with tape. Sew around side and bottom edges using ¼" (6mm) seams. Clip curves and turn right side out. Finger press seams and weight with a book to set. Thread ball chain through eyelets and make a bow at top, securing "knot" with wire. Wrap wire around each loop of bow to keep it in shape, hide ends in back. For hanger, cut a 7" (18cm) piece of ball chain and stitch ends to inside back edge of stocking top.

Holiday Goodies Stocking

Christmas is the time of year for an abundance of sweets and on this stocking I've re-created my favorites—candy canes, gingerbread men, and peppermint candies. Made from felt and seasonal colors of fabric paint, this stocking is simply delicious.

MATERIALS

½ yd (45.5cm) of medium brown felt

Square each of dark brown, green, and red felt

White and red fabric paint

1 pkg white jumbo rickrack

1 yd (91.5cm) of red-and-white check ribbon, ⅞" (2cm) wide

Fabric glue

Sewing thread

Enlarge stocking pattern (page 35), adding ¼" (6mm) seam allowance on sides and bottom and 1" (2.5cm) hem allowance on top. Cut two stocking pieces from medium brown felt. Sew side and bottom seams. Clip curves and turn right side out. Fold top hem to inside and glue in place. Glue white rickrack inside edge of stocking front. Trace trim pieces (page 44), and cut three gingerbread men from dark brown felt, three each round candies and candy canes from red felt, and three round candies from green felt. Work details on trims with white paint, adding red

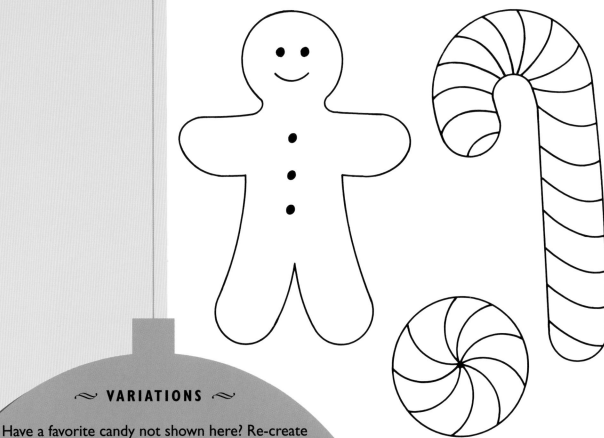

Patterns shown at 100%

painted buttons to gingerbread

men. Arrange and glue trims to

stocking front. For hanging bow,

make two 4½" (11.5cm) loops from

ribbon; gather centers of loops. Cut a small

piece of ribbon and sew over gathered area. Fold re-

maining ribbon in half and tack bow 3½" (9cm) below fold. Stitch

bow and loop to back edge of stocking top.

Menswear Stocking

Starkly simple in fine gray wool

and gold blazer buttons, this stocking would suit

a Fortune 500 CEO, and will add

a quietly sophisticated touch to your

holiday festivities.

Enlarge and cut out stocking front pattern pieces (page 47) (seam allowances are included). For stocking back, enlarge general stocking pattern adding ¼" (6mm) seam allowances to sides and bottom, 1" (2.5cm) hem allowance to top edge. From wool, cut one of each pattern piece. With machine set on medium zigzag, stitch edge of upper hem allowances on all three stocking pieces. With machine set on straight stitch and with right sides together, stitch two front pieces together along centerline to flap, using a ¼" (6mm) seam. Steam press the seam to the larger (right) side, pressing flap to the same side along fold line. Fold and press top hems to inside along fold line. Open folds on right side of front and miter the allowances to the corner. Pin flaps together and with machine set on zigzag again, stitch bottom and sides of flap together as far as possible. Return machine to straight stitch. With right sides facing, pin front of stocking to back at side and bottom, and stitch using a ¼" (6mm) seam. Clip curves and turn right side out, steam pressing seams flat and hem allowances to inside. Slipstitch hem allowance to inside. Sew buttons evenly spaced, approximately ⅜" (1cm) from edge and ⅜" (1cm) apart on flap, through both layers. For hanger, cut a strip of wool 1½" × 8" (4 × 20.5cm). Zigzag raw edges. Fold and press long edges to center. Hand stitch in place or use fusible adhesive. Fold in half and stitch by hand or machine to inside back edge of stocking.

∼ VARIATIONS ∼

This stocking is more limited in possible variations, but take a look at the suiting fabrics available. Try a pinstripe or a houndstooth check. You might also try making a white stocking liner with its shaft lengthened enough to fold back and still extend ¾" to 1" (2 to 2.5cm) above the stocking to give the appearance of a sleeve cuff.

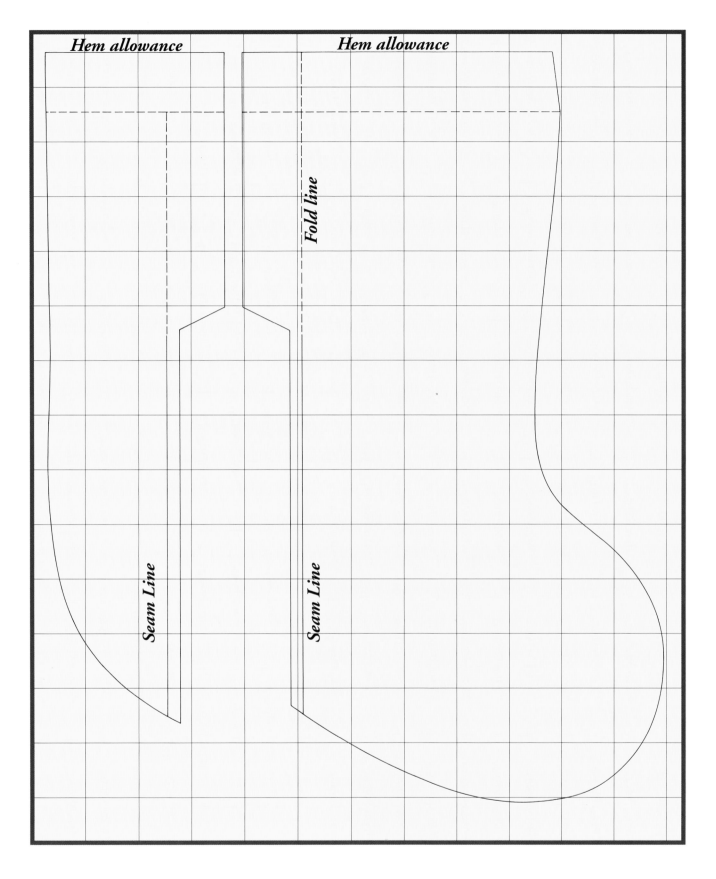

Hem allowance

Hem allowance

Fold line

Seam Line

Seam Line

Front pattern pieces
1 square = 1 inch
Enlarge to 208%

Dinosaurs Galore Stocking

What dinosaur lover wouldn't be

charmed by this stocking? Simple shapes cut

from felt and highlighted by minimal embroidery

will make this a favorite.

MATERIALS

½ yd (45.5cm) of gray felt

Squares of felt in assorted colors (I used 3 each of red and green and 2 each of blue and purple)

Liquid fusible adhesive

Embroidery floss in shades of red, blue, and purple to contrast with gray felt

Sewing thread

Enlarge stocking pattern (page 35), adding ¼" (6mm) seam allowances all around. Cut two stocking pieces from gray felt. Trace dinosaur and shrubbery patterns (page 51), adding seam allowances where pieces meet edge of stocking, and cut from desired colors of felt. Arrange dinosaur on stocking front as shown, layering dinosaurs and shrubs to cover awkward edges. Layer stegosaurus over his plates. Layer of back plates will be fused flat to felt, but only the bottom edges of top layer of plates will be fused so there will be some dimension to the design. When the arrangement is satisfactory, apply liquid fusible adhesive to backs of dinosaurs and shrubs and place on stocking front. Following manufacturer's directions, fuse all the felt shapes in place. Using three strands of coordinating embroidery floss, work dinosaurs' facial details according to pattern. Cut tree fronds for top edge from felt, using patterns on this page or cutting freehand from several shades of green. Pin fronds to top edge as desired; baste in place. Cut a strip of green felt 1¼" × 16" (3 × 5cm), piecing if necessary. Fold strip lengthwise, not quite in half, but having one side slightly wider than the other. Place over top edge of stocking, pinning narrower side to front of stocking, overlapping fronds. Stitch close to

Tree fronds
Patterns shown at 100%

edge on front, making sure you are catching back edge at same time.

For hanger, cut a strip of felt 1½" × 7" (4 × 18cm). Fold long edges of strip to center and topstitch ⅛" (3mm) from fold. Fold strip in half and sew ends securely to inside back edge of stocking top.

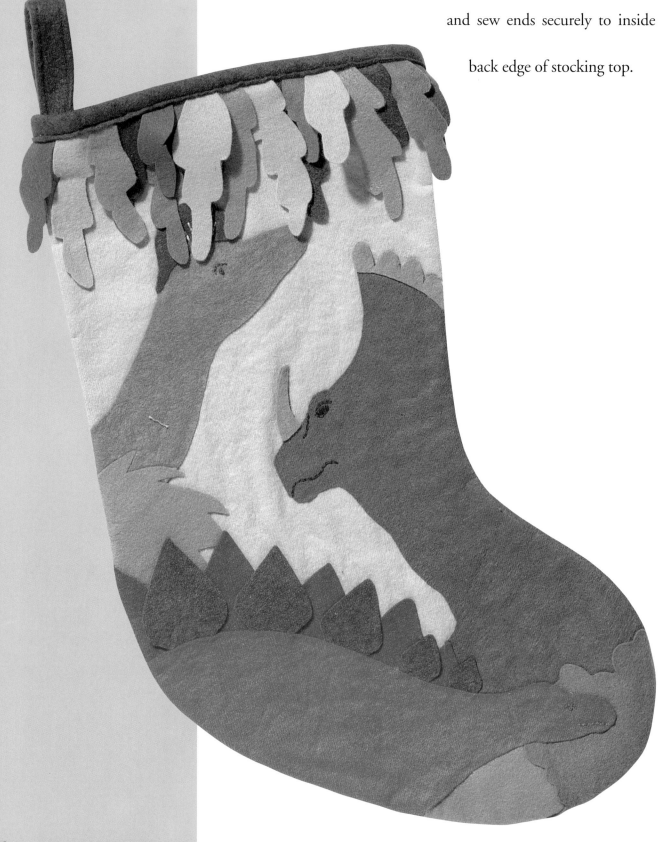

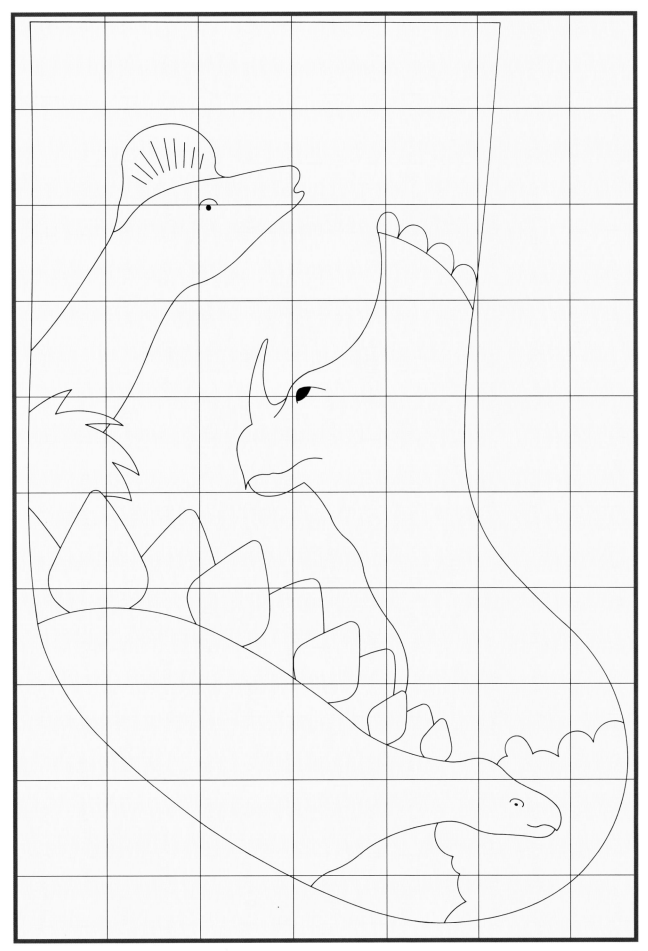

Enlarge to 154%

1 square = 1 inch
Dinosaur and shrubbery Patterns

Cool & Contemporary

Basketweave Plaid Stocking

Strips of plaids in holiday colors were woven together to create this countryish stocking cuffed in unbleached cotton batting for a charming and casual look.

MATERIALS

½ yd (45.5cm) each predominantly green and red plaid fabric

½ yd (45.5cm) of muslin

½ yd (45.5cm) of red fabric

½ yd (45.5cm) of lightweight fusible interfacing

11" (28cm) square unbleached cotton batting

11" (28cm) square paper backed fusible adhesive

Matching threads

½" (1.5cm) bias tape maker

Enlarge and trace stocking pattern (page 35) twice to back (nonfuse side) of fusible interfacing, taking care to flop the pattern to create mirror images (front and back of stocking). Cut out, leaving at least ¾" (2cm) all around. Cut plaids into relatively equal strips (I cut along center of red and green striped portion of plaids), cutting lengthwise strips 16" (40.5cm) long and crosswise strips 12" (30.5cm) long. Lay one interfacing piece fusible side up onto an ironing board. Pin lengthwise strips, butting against one another, approximately ½" (1.5cm) above top edge of stocking outline. Make sure you have cut and pinned enough strips to completely cover shape with at least ½" (1.5cm) to spare on all sides. Weave crosswise strips over and under lengthwise strips, again covering entire shape plus at least ½" (1.5cm) beyond all sides. Pin any strips necessary to ease weaving, and when sizable amounts have been woven "baste fuse" in place with steam iron according to manufacturer's directions. When weaving is completed, turn stocking piece over and fuse permanently according to manufacturer's directions. Repeat with remaining stocking piece.

Trace stocking pattern twice to muslin again reversing once to create mirror images. With ruler, mark back of each piece into 1" (2.5cm) squares set on a 45-degree angle to top edge of stocking. Pin each marked muslin piece to back of woven piece and pin around outside edges. Stitch along marked lines with coordinating or contrasting thread. Pin pieces right sides together matching traced outlines (stitching line) and cut out ¼" (6mm) beyond lines.

From red fabric cut three 1⅛" (3cm) bias strips and one 1" (2.5cm) strip. Stitch two 1⅛" (3cm) strips together. Pin stocking pieces wrong sides together with one raw edge of long bias strip even with raw edge of stocking front. Stitch using a ¼" (6mm) seam. Fold bias strip to back, folding under ¼" (6mm) along raw edge and slipstitch to back over seam line.

Trace stocking cuff pattern twice to paper backing of fusible adhesive again flopping piece to create front and back pieces (mirror images). Fuse to back of muslin according to manufacturer's directions and cut out, cutting ¼" (6mm) beyond marked lines. Fuse to back of unbleached cotton batting and cut out. Sew side seams. Use remaining 1⅛" (3cm) wide bias strip to stitch over bottom edge of cuff, same as for stocking body. Overlap ends on back of cuff. Turn cuff right side out and matching center front to center front, pin cuff inside top edge of stocking, having right side of cuff facing wrong side of stocking. Sew cuff/stocking seam. Fold cuff to outside.

Pull remaining bias strip (1"[2.5cm] wide) through bias tape maker and iron to set folds, or fold both long edges to center and press. Fold strip in half again lengthwise and slipstitch folded edge together (you will need a piece about 8"[2.5] long). For hanger, cut strip to length desired and securely stitch ends to inside back edge of stocking.

∼ VARIATIONS ∼

This stocking was woven from coordinating plaids, but why not try contrasting solids? If you cut the strips in varying widths a truly interesting checked look would form beneath your fingers. Your options are limited only by the fabrics available in your scrap basket or fabric store.

Stained Glass Stocking

MATERIALS

½ yd (45.5cm) of white cotton fabric

Assorted scraps of brightly colored taffeta (we used teal, bright and dark blues, and dark green)

Small amount paper-backed fusible adhesive

3-D foiling glue

Gold foil for use with foiling glue

1 yd (91.5cm) of narrow gold cording

Sewing thread

Note: There are several foiling systems available in craft stores today. Make your choice depending on the availability and ease of use and follow the manufacturer's directions. Basically the kits consist of a glue and the foil. The glue is applied to the project and must be allowed to dry to a certain tackiness, which may take as long as 24 hours. Then the foil is laid over the glue and rubbed into all the cracks and crevices to aid adherence. Some systems have a finish coat that enables you to wash the project, although stockings don't usually require laundering.

Inspired by glorious stained glass windows designed by Frank Lloyd Wright, this stocking uses gold foil and three-dimensional foiling glue to achieve the leaded effect of real stained glass.

Enlarge stocking pattern (page 35), adding ¼" (6mm) seam allowances on sides and bottom and 1" (2.5cm) hem allowance at top. Cut four stocking pieces from white cotton. Transfer stained glass design (page 59) onto right side of one stocking piece. Following photo or working from your own design, trace selected stained glass motifs onto paper back of fusible adhesive. Following manufacturer's directions, fuse to taffeta scraps and cut out. Fuse motifs in place to stocking front. When you are satisfied with the amount of color on stocking front, apply foiling glue to all lines, extending lines into seam allowances. After glue has dried, apply foil, carefully rubbing it into all corners and curves of glued lines.

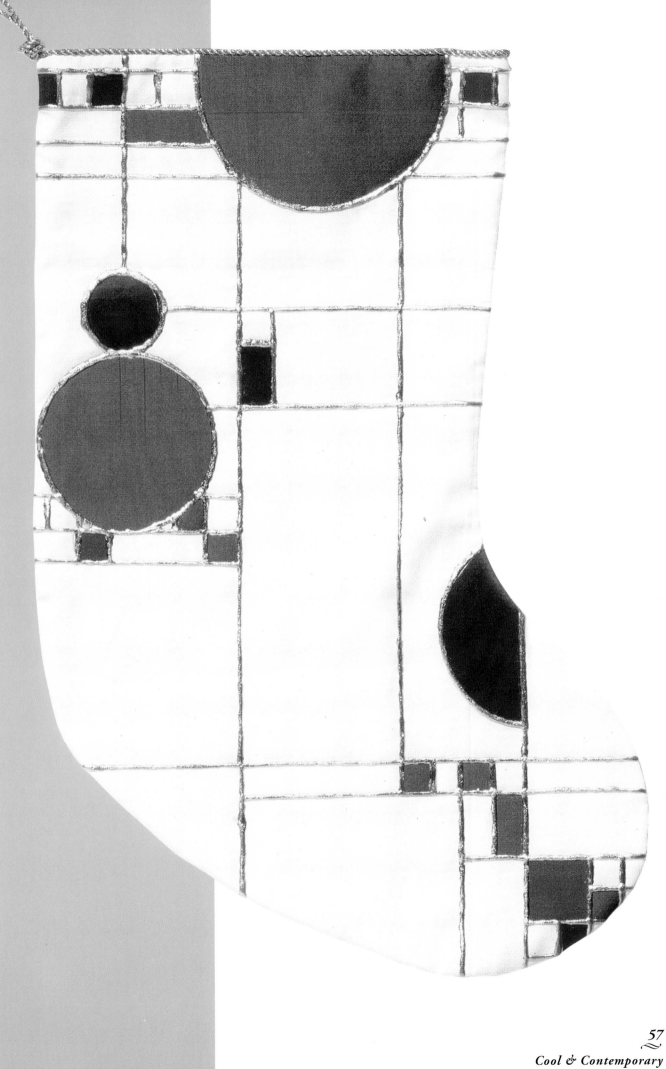

This stocking was inspired by a Frank Lloyd Wright design found in a catalog, but there are any number of pieces of stained glass that could serve as your inspiration. Churches and museums offer many examples, as do museum catalogs. Regular fabric paint in a squeeze-type applicator can be substituted for the foil "leading" used here, as could an applied cord. You could also try cutting the colored "glass" pieces from felt and gluing them to a black (felt or other fabric of your choice) background to achieve another sort of stained glass look.

You will now assemble the stocking using two pieces for both the front and back to give the stocking added stability. Lay stocking front, right side up, on top of one white stocking piece. Place remaining two pieces on top of stocking front and pin side and bottom edges. Avoid putting pins into foiled glue lines. Sew around sides and bottom using a ¼" (6mm) seam and zigzag around top edges. Clip curves and carefully turn right side out. Fold top hem to inside and slipstitch in place. Hand sew gold cord along top edge of stocking, knotting a hanging loop and tacking it in place when you reach the back.

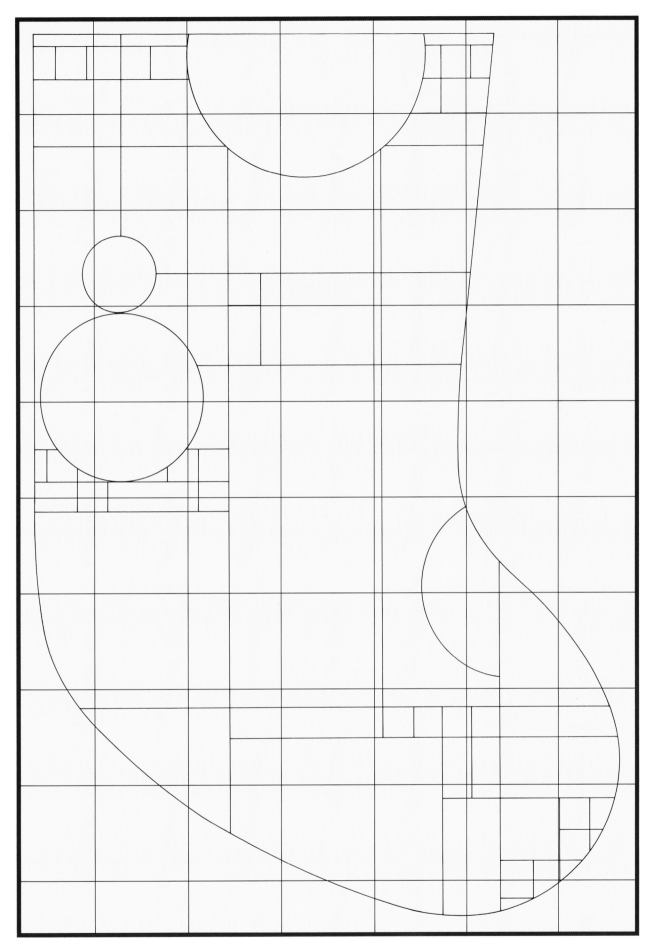

Enlarge to 158%

Stained glass design pattern
1 square = 1 inch

Starry Night Stocking

Glittering gold and silver stars

like those guiding Santa's sleigh on

Christmas Eve twinkle against black felt to

lend an air of sophistication to this

simply elegant stocking.

½ yd (45.5cm) of black felt

Small amounts of gold and silver lamé

Small amount of paper-backed fusible adhesive

Gold or silver machine embroidery thread and black sewing thread

Craft knife or small sharp scissors

Fabric glue

Trace stocking pattern (page 35) and cuff pattern (page 63), adding seam allowances of ¼" (6mm) on sides and bottom of stocking and ½" (1.5cm) hem on top; add the same allowances only to the sides and top of cuff. Bottom hem allowance is already included. Cut out two stocking and cuff pieces from felt. Draw star shapes on paper backing of fusible adhesive (I used four large, seven medium, and twelve small stars). Using lowest heat setting possible and a press cloth between fabric and iron, fuse to back of lamé. Cut out stars and position on stocking and cuff fronts letting some fall partially into seam allowances to give the appearance that the design continues around the stocking. Portions of some stars should also fall into the bottom hem allowance on the cuff. Using lowest setting and press cloth again, fuse stars to stocking and cuff fronts.

With machine threaded with gold or silver on top and black in bobbin and set for narrow satin stitch, sew around edges of stars. Using a craft knife or a very sharp pair of scissors, carefully cut along the edges of portions of stars extending into cuff's bottom hem allowance. Fold hem to inside and glue in place.

With right sides together, sew around stocking sides and bottom using ¼" (6mm) seams. Repeat with cuff. Clip curves and turn stocking and cuff right side out. With right side of cuff facing wrong side of stocking, place cuff inside stocking, aligning side seams and top edges, and stitch using a ⅜" (1cm) seam. Turn cuff to

∾ VARIATIONS ∾

A flurry of white and/or silver snowflakes on a blue background might be a visually striking variation on this stocking. Fold paper, just as you did when you were a kid, to cut symmetrical snowflakes for patterns. You might also try an arrangement of suns and moons, with or without stars. As an alternative to cutting out the motifs and appliquéing them to the background fabric, you could also try rubber stamping them. Designs for a snowflake, sun, moon, and stars are all available as rubber stamps, and using one of the available metallic ink stamp pads would create a dramatic effect. If you choose to explore this route, I would suggest not having the motifs overhang the cuff as I did here. You will also find some applicable tips in the instructions for the Special Message Stocking in chapter four.

outside. For hanger, cut a 1½" × 7" (4 × 18cm) strip of felt. Fold long edges to center and sew in place. Fold strip in half and sew securely to inside back edge of stocking top.

Cuff

Pattern shown at 100%

Chapter Three
~ ~ ~ ~ ~ ~
# Victorian Elegance

*T*he toe of the stocking shape featured in this chapter is slim, with a silhouette that is rather Victorian in feel. This shape is elegant and refined—ideal for all those luxurious fabrics you have stashed away for something special. Velvets, satins, and lace, along with beads and fancy trims come together here to create elaborate masterpieces like those the Victorians were experts at creating. Crazy quilts, for example, were a favorite with Victorian women—what better way to show off one's needlework? Here you'll find an easy method of achieving a similar look without investing a lengthy amount of time in hand embroidery. You'll also see how ecru lace over satin produces a stocking with a bridal feel, while the Chinese silk brocade I stumbled across one day recalls the mysterious Orient with which the Victorians were so fascinated.

General stocking pattern for chapter
Enlarge to 153%

Chinese Silk Brocade Stocking

MATERIALS

½ yd (45.5m) of Chinese silk brocade

½ yd (45.5cm) of contrasting lightweight fabric for piping and lining

1½ yds (1.4m) of narrow cord for piping

9 buttons to cover, size 24 (⅝" [1.5cm] diameter)

Matching sewing thread

The minute I spotted this brocade

I pictured the stocking as it now appears—

very elegant, piped in vibrant green and buttoned

up the side like the traditional garments

of the Far East.

Enlarge general pattern (page 65), and stocking front pattern (page 69), adding ¼" (6mm) seam allowances all around. Cut one of each stocking piece from silk brocade. On contrasting fabric, find and mark the bias, from one corner to opposite side. Cut two bias strips 1" (2.5cm) wide by the width of the fabric. Using general stocking pattern, cut two from remaining fabric.

With cording or zipper foot on machine, lay cord down center of one bias strip, fold bias strip in half over cord and sew close to cord. On right front stocking piece, lay piping along right side of center edge with raw edges even. Sew piping to center front edge and around top corner. Do not cut piping; leave it hanging to complete top edge later. Fold both long edges of remaining bias strip to center and fold strip in half lengthwise, enclosing raw edges. By hand, blind stitch folded edges together. Cut bias strip into nine 2½" (6.5cm) pieces for button loops. Fold raw edges of piping and stocking seam allowance on center front edge to inside. Pin button loops evenly spaced along piped edge with raw edges of button loops even with raw edges of piping, and tack in place.

Overlap right front stocking over left front stocking piece, pin, and carefully stitch in the ditch (along the seam) between piping and right front stocking piece. Pin completed stocking front to back, with right sides together, and sew along sides and bottom using a ¼" (6mm) seam. Clip curves and turn right side out. Finish applying piping around top edge of stocking ending behind right front corner. Fold piping up and seam allowances to inside.

With right sides together, sew lining pieces together using ⅜" (1cm) seam. Trim seam allowances to ³⁄₁₆" (5mm). Fold ⅜" (1cm) around top edge of lining to wrong side. Slip lining inside stocking and blind stitch folded edge to piping seam around top of stocking. Following manufacturer's directions, cover buttons with brocade. Sew buttons to left front

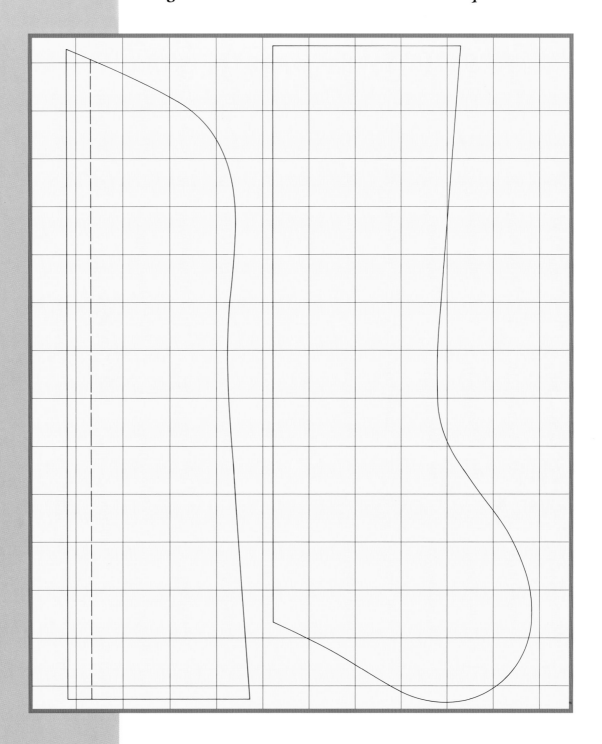

opposite button loops. For hanger, cut a 1¾" × 6" (4.5 × 15cm) strip of

lining fabric. Fold long edges to center and bring folded edges together

to enclose raw edges. Blind stitch folded edges together. Fold under raw

ends and sew securely to inside back edge of stocking top.

Flower Trimmed Stocking

Vibrant silk flowers tacked to the cuff of a plain ivory velveteen stocking transform it into an exquisite holiday decoration.

MATERIALS

½ yd (45.5cm) of ivory velveteen

Assorted silk flowers

2 yds (1.8m) of purple velvet ribbon, 1" (2.5cm) wide

Matching sewing thread

Enlarge stocking pattern (page 65) and cuff pattern (page 72), adding seam allowances of ¼" (6mm) to sides and bottom and ½" (1.5cm) to top. Cut two stocking and four cuff pieces from velveteen. With right sides together, sew stocking side and bottom edges, and each set of cuff pieces together using ¼" (6mm) seams. Trim curves on stocking and turn it and one set of cuff pieces right side out. Place cuff pieces one inside the other, right sides together, and sew bottom seam. Turn cuff right side out and place inside stocking, aligning side seams and top edges. Sew cuff to stocking using a ⅜" (1cm) seam. Fold cuff to outside.

Stitch flowers to cuff in a pleasing arrangement. To make a bow and hanger, make two loops with ribbon, each about 6" (15cm) across. Cut a 2" (5cm) piece of ribbon and wrap around center of loops, tacking in place. Fold remaining ribbon in half and tack bow to ribbon 4" (10cm) below fold. Stitch bow to back edge of stocking top. Trim ends as desired.

Cuff

Pattern shown at 100%

Dad's Old Ties

A few old ties lifted from your husband's wardrobe or purchased from the local thrift shop will be elevated to elegant new heights when coordinated with metallic trims and turned into this stocking with a crazy-quilt look.

MATERIALS

½ yd (45.5cm) of muslin

12" × 18" (30.5 × 45.5cm) piece of burgundy velveteen or other material for stocking back

Approximately 7 men's ties

½ yd (45.5cm) each of 6 gold trims (or more depending on number of ties used)

2 yds (1.8m) of medium-width gold cord

Nylon monofilament thread for machine sewing

Liquid Pins (water-soluble basting glue)

Seam binding

Note: Tie fabrics are very slippery, so use many pins.

Enlarge stocking pattern (page 65), adding seam allowances of ¼" (6mm) on sides and bottom and 1" (2.5cm) hem allowance on top. Open back seam on all ties, removing any lining and interfacing. Decide on the arrangement of ties, alternating thick and thin ends to end up with a fairly square arrangement. Cut a piece of muslin 18" (45.5cm) square. Beginning with first tie at one side of arrangement, trim excess fabric to ¼" (6mm) on either side of front panel (you will be sewing along fold line). Press first tie open and pin to one edge of muslin. Baste along each edge of tie. Open up second tie, press, and

trim excess fabric in the same manner as for first. Remembering to reverse thick and thin ends, pin second tie on top of first tie, with right sides together and raw edges even. Baste second tie in place along pinned edge. Press second tie piece back over seam, pin, and baste second edge flat to muslin. Continue trimming and adding ties until muslin is fairly well covered.

Glue gold trims over seams between ties. When glue has dried, set machine for medium-width zigzag stitch, thread top with nylon thread, and stitch down center of each gold trim.

Cut out stocking front from assembled piece. Cut out stocking back from velveteen. With right sides together, baste front to back along sides an bottom using ¼" (6mm) seams. Machine stitch over basting. Clip curves and turn stocking right side out. Stitch seam binding to top edge, fold hem to inside, and sew seam binding in place by hand. Beginning at front seam, hand stitch gold cord along side seams. Make a loop for hanger when you reach top back edge, then continue stitching cord around top edge of stocking.

∼ VARIATIONS ∼

This stocking is designed in a very simple type of crazy quilt work. The next step from here would be to cut the ties in random blocks, piecing them in the same overlapping manner described here and sewing over the seams with decorative machine stitching, using a metallic or other glitzy machine embroidery thread. If you have the time and patience, a piece of traditional crazy quilt work makes a truly impressive stocking. Assemble the blocks of tie or other luxury-type fabrics on a lightweight muslin base, and embroider over the seams in a variety of hand-worked embroidery stitches, using contrasting cotton and silk threads.

Satin and Lace Stocking

Looking as rich and unique as a heirloom wedding gown, this stocking of heavy lace over ivory satin will look very sophisticated among your holiday decorations.

MATERIALS

½ yd (45.5cm) of lace with scalloped edging

½ yd (45.5cm) of ivory colored satin

Approximately 30 sequins in various shades of gold

Approximately 30 small pearl beads

Matching sewing thread

Enlarge stocking pattern (page 65), adding seam allowances of ¼" (6mm) to sides and bottom and ½" (1.5cm) at top edges. Cut two stocking pieces each from lace and satin, taking care to leave at least 6" (15cm) of lace at scalloped edge for cuff. With right sides of lace together between right sides of satin, pin and sew around side and bottom edges using a ¼" (6mm) seam. If you experience any difficulty sewing this "sandwich" together, you may need to baste the lace pieces to the satin pieces before sewing seam. Clip curves and turn stocking right side out; press seams flat. Baste top edges together.

Trace cuff pattern (page 78) for scalloped cuff. Lay scalloped edge of lace along bottom edge of cuff pattern. With points of scallops just touching the line and centered along the available space, trace scallops.

Add ¼" (6mm) seam allowance beyond scallops and on sides and 1"

(2.5cm) seam allowance on top. Cut four cuff pieces from satin. With

right sides together, sew two cuff pieces together at a time along bot-

tom edge. Clip curves and corners and turn right side out. Press seams

flat. Position lace on right side of cuff pieces, lining up scallops and

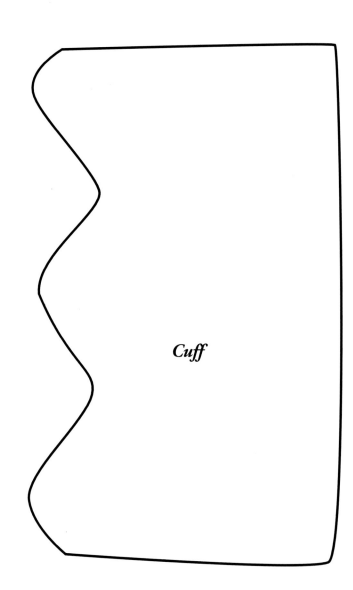

Cuff

Pattern shown at 100%

having lace approximately ³⁄₁₆" (5mm) above bottom edge. Pin or baste lace in place to cuff front only and trim top and side edges. Open cuffs and with right sides together, pin cuff sections along side seams, matching bottom seam and edges of lace. Stitch side seams and turn cuff right side out. Baste top edges together. With right side of cuff facing wrong side of stocking, sew cuff to stocking using a ³⁄₈" (1cm) seam. Fold cuff to right side.

Sew sequins held in place by small pearl beads to highlight scalloped edge of lace cuff. For hanger, cut a 1¼" × 8" (3 × 20.5cm) strip each of lace and satin. Place lace on top of satin and zigzag edges together. Fold long edges ¼" (6mm) to back and stitch in place. Fold strip in half and sew ends securely to inside back edge of stocking top.

∼ VARIATIONS ∼

Depending on the lace selected for this particular stocking, individual motifs on the lace could be beaded or embellished with sequins and other decorative trims. The cuff assembly could be simplified by eliminating the scallops and embellishing the resulting straight lower edge with fringe or tassels

Charmed Stocking

Gold charms gathered over the years were brought out of

a storage bin to hang from the small gold bows

on this dark green silk taffeta stocking.

E nlarge stocking pattern (page 65) and trace to fusible interfacing twice, flopping pattern to make one each for front
and back. Cut out with approximately ½" (1.5cm) extra all around
and fuse to back of green taffeta. Using stocking pattern, cut out
one stocking front and back from fused taffeta adding ¼" (6mm)
seam allowance all around. Pin stocking front to back, right sides
together and sew sides and bottom using ¼" (6mm) seam. Clip
curves and turn right side out, pressing seams flat. Cut nine 10"
(25.5cm) lengths of gold braid and tie into bows in this fashion:
form two loops either side of center point, place one loop over
other loop and draw one under and through, tying loops in single

MATERIALS

½ yd (45.5cm) of green silk taffeta

½ yd (45.5cm) of lining fabric

½ yd (45.5cm) of fusible interfacing

2 yds (1.8m) of gold cord

*Approximately 3 yds (2.7m) of assorted
gold braids or trims*

9 gold-tone charms

*9 gold-tone jingle bells, same size or
assorted*

Thread

knot. Arrange and pin bows in place on stocking front, then tack each in place, adding a charm just below the knot of each bow. Tack jingle bells between and around bows.

From lining fabric, cut two stocking shapes adding ³⁄₁₆" (5mm) seam allowance on sides and bottom, ¼" (6mm) on top edge. Stitch around sides and bottom edges using a ¼" (6mm) seam. Slip stocking into lining (right sides together) and pin top edges together having raw edges even. Stitch along front edge and just past side seams on each side. Leave remaining back edge open to turn stocking right side out. Slip lining inside stocking, turn under remaining raw edges on opening and slip-stitch together.

Slipstitch gold cord to side seams, working down front edge, around bottom and up back seam before working around top edge of stocking. Cut a 6" (15cm) length of gold trim for hanger, sew ends to inside back edge of stocking top.

Hanging Fern Stocking

Looking ethereal, these coiled and hanging fronds are surreal depictions of the ferns that flourished near the porch steps of the house where I grew up. They make very untraditional decorations for this unique stocking.

½ yd (45.5cm) of light green organza

½ yd (45.5cm) of light- to medium-weight chartreuse fabric

2 yds (1.8m) of silver cord

Matching sewing thread, plus blue-green, green, and silver machine embroidery thread

Fabric marker (either pencil or disappearing marker)

To make the applied trims for this stocking, you need to cover the silver cord with satin stitching. Thread bobbin with matching thread (bobbin will be threaded with thread matching the fabric throughout), use blue-green thread on top, and set machine on medium-width satin stitch (stitch width should cover cord from side to side). Place cord under presser foot, leaving about 1" (2.5cm) extending from the back. Begin stitching and with one hand behind, slowly pull cord through as it is covered. It is all right if coverage is a little uneven—the silver showing through will complement the finished design. Cover the length of cord with stitching, or cut the cord

into two lengths and cover each separately if you prefer working with shorter lengths of cord.

Find and mark a line along the bias on the organza from one corner to opposite side of fabric. Mark five more lines each ½" (1.5cm) away from the last. With machine set on slightly narrower satin stitch and same threads in machine, stitch along every other marked line. Don't worry if stitching lines ripple. Switch blue-green thread for green thread, and stitch in the same way along remaining lines. Cut strips out as close to stitching as you can without nicking stitching. (You will have three strips with stitching along both sides of each.)

Enlarge stocking pattern (page 65), adding seam allowances of ¼" (6mm) on side and bottom edges and 1" (2.5cm) on top. Cut two each from organza and chartreuse fabrics. By hand, baste one organza stocking piece to each chartreuse stocking piece, making sure you reverse one to make a front and back piece. On front, lightly mark placement of ferns with pencil or fabric marker following the pattern on page 86. With machine set on straight stitch and threaded on top with green thread, stitch along marked lines on right side of stocking front. Thread top with silver, set machine for narrow zigzag, and stitch near green stitching and along additional lines marked for silver stitching. Coil

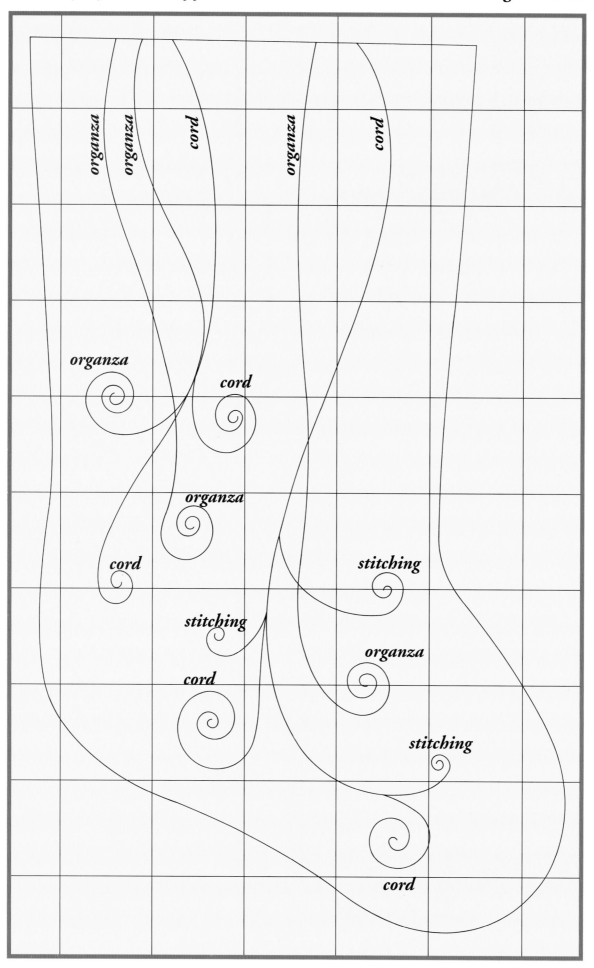

and hand stitch covered cord in place near and over green and silver stitching. Don't follow stitched lines exactly; reveal some silver here and green there to create an arty effect.

Working down the approximate center line of organza strips, coil and hand sew them in place according to layout (page 86). Make a little gather here and there as desired for a fluted effect. On the left side of stocking, apply next two strips of organza in the same manner along marked lines. After organza has been applied, sew decorative stitching for cord ferns, as for right side of stocking, this time sewing on top of applied organza. Apply cord on or near stitching in the same manner as before.

With right sides together, sew stocking front to back along sides and bottom using ¼" (6mm) seams. Clip curves and turn right side out. Machine baste ¼" (6mm) from top edge. Fold ¼" (6mm) at top edge to wrong side along basting. Fold again ½" (1.5cm) away from first fold, enclosing raw edges and slipstitch in place. For hanger, cut a 1¾" × 6" (4.5 × 15cm) strip each of organza and chartreuse fabrics. Place organza over chartreuse and baste along edges. Fold long edges to center, bring folded edges together, and stitch in place. Fold in half and sew ends securely to inside back edge of stocking top.

∼ VARIATIONS ∼

By working with fabrics from the blue and teal families when creating this stocking and adding a few more motifs to fill it out, you can achieve an effect more along the lines of a peacock's tail, rather than the ferns suggested by the greens I used. Additional use of sequins, beads, and other trims could make the stocking more ornate and luxurious.

Beaded Nylon and Taffeta Stocking

Pleated sheer black nylon and

a shimmer of iridescent beads tame the shocking

pink taffeta they cover to create this elegantly

feminine stocking topped with a luxurious

black velvet and bead-adorned cuff.

Enlarge stocking pattern (page 65), adding ¼" (6mm) seam allowances all around, and cut two each from pink taffeta and pleated nylon. Sandwich the nylon pieces between the taffeta and sew around sides and bottom using a ¼" (6mm) seam. Clip curves and turn right side out, finger pressing the seams flat.

Adding ¼" (6mm) seam allowance to sides and bottom and ½" (1.5cm) to top of cuff pattern (page 72), cut two cuff pieces each from velvet and lining fabrics. With right sides together, and using ¼" (6mm) seams, sew two velvet pieces together at side seams. Repeat with lining pieces. With right sides together and side seams aligned, stitch lining to

~ VARIATIONS ~

The combination of colors in this stocking

can be varied in a number of ways. When shopping

for fabrics, try layering different color combinations of

chiffon and background fabrics to judge the effect.

Metallic organza would create a very interesting effect

over a bold, dramatic shade of taffeta or satin. If you

enjoy beadwork, try beading a motif or initial

on the body of the stocking.

velvet at bottom edges. Turn right side out and machine baste top edges together. With right side of cuff facing wrong side of stocking, pin top edges together and stitch using a ¼" (6mm) seam. Fold cuff to outside.

Thread needle with double length of thread and anchor at one edge of stocking approximately 1" (2.5cm) under cuff. Working along the seam line, pick up a bead and secure it to seam. Bring needle up again ¼" (6mm) away and pick up another bead. Continue in this fashion around the outside edge of stocking, finishing under cuff on opposite side. Cut cuff beading guide from paper and pin to edge of cuff with bottom of curves ⅝" (1.5cm) above bottom of cuff. Thread needle with double length of thread and secure on lining side of cuff at some point along the pattern. Bring needle to the front and pick up a bead. Secure bead with a couple of stitches through both layers of fabric and bring needle to the front again ⅛" (3mm) farther along pattern. Continue working in this fashion until entire cuff has been completed.

For hanger, fold ribbon in half and tack securely to inside back edge of stocking top.

Elegant Woven Ribbons Stocking

Looking far more complicated than it actually is, rich burgundy ribbons in a variety of textures have been woven together and accented with gold to create this elegant stocking.

Enlarge stocking pattern (page 65) to paper.
Mark stocking shape into a 1" (2.5cm) grid set at a 45-degree angle to the stocking top edge. This grid will help you to keep the ribbon weaving on a straight grain. On ironing board, lay fusible interfacing, fusible side up, on top of stocking pattern. Using a straight pin in each corner, pin to ironing board cover. Working in one direction and starting somewhere in the middle of the stocking shape, cut ribbons into lengths to cover shape with approximately 1" (2.5cm) extra for seam allowance on either side. Pin ribbons in place on interfacing (you can simply poke

MATERIALS

Approximately 10 yds (9m) assorted ribbons (You will need 6 kinds of ribbons. Get more of the ribbons you like the most.)

1 yd (91.5cm) of gold rickrack

14" × 18" (35.5 × 45.5cm) of fusible interfacing

½ yd (45.5cm) of backing/lining fabric

2 yds (1.8m) of 4mm gold rope braid

Fabric glue (optional)

Ironing board with pinnable cover

Iron

pins at an angle into ironing board cover to hold them while you work).

When you have one direction covered, start working the other direction, weaving crosswise ribbons over and under those already pinned down. Remove pins as needed to facilitate weaving.

When you are satisfied with your woven ribbons and the entire stocking shape is covered with adequate seam allowances (check the areas where ribbons overlap for interfacing show through), cover with damp press cloth and steam with iron to fuse ribbons in place to interfacing. Remove pins and fuse outer edges of ribbons, taking care not to fuse press cloth to interfacing. Cut out stocking shape adding ¼" (6mm) seam allowances all around. If necessary, glue any ends of ribbon that seam to be loose.

From backing/lining fabric cut three stocking shapes with the same seam allowances. Sew two lining pieces together along sides and bottom with a ⅜" (1cm) seam. Trim seam allowances to 3⁄16" (5mm). Pin backing piece to ribbon stocking, right sides together and sew around side and bottom edges with a ¼" (6mm) seam. Clip curves and turn right side out. From back, carefully press seams flat.

On both stocking and lining, turn ¼" (6mm) around top edge to wrong side. Slip lining inside stocking and pin top edges together. Slipstitch folded edges together. Starting at top front edge of stocking, slipstitch gold cord down front seam and up back seam. At top of back seam, form hanging loop with cord and tack in place, then continue sewing cord around top edge of stocking, ending back at hanging loop.

∾ VARIATIONS ∾

The wide variety of ribbons available in your notions store is the only limit to the variations you can create on this particular idea. Go Tyrolean with floral braids and red and green ribbons, or bold and colorful with several bright colors, polka dots, and checks.

Chapter Four

~ ~ ~ ~ ~

New Traditions

*T*his final gathering of stockings is cut from a very classic, traditional pattern. Round of toe and heel, the shape presented here is most commonly associated with the holidays. Depending on one's choice of materials, any one of these stockings would be equally at home in a country cabin or stately manor house. Rich burgundy velvet quilted with gold thread and embellished with pearls results in a majestic stocking, while a stark, simple version in two contrasting colors of embossed velvet makes a bold statement anywhere. On a more informal note, an excerpt from your favorite Christmas story rubber stamped on muslin and trimmed with rickrack will make for a very personalized stocking.

General stocking pattern for chapter
Enlarge to 151%

Embossed Velvet Stocking

Luxurious velvet embossed with

dramatic stars and fanciful squiggles

makes for a bold stocking that needs no further

embellishment—unless you'd like to add a

name in gold metallic thread on the cuff.

MATERIALS

½ yd (45.5cm) of embossed green velvet

12" (30.5cm) square of embossed red velvet

12" (30.5cm) square of red fabric for cuff lining

Matching sewing thread

Note: Velvet has a tendency to slip when sewn by machine. It is frequently necessary to hand baste seams before machine stitching

Enlarge stocking pattern (page 95) and cuff pattern (page 98), adding ¼" (6mm) seam allowance on sides and bottoms and ½" (1.5cm) on tops. Cut two stocking pieces from green velvet, two cuff pieces from red velvet, and two cuff lining pieces from red fabric. With right sides together, sew sides and bottom of stocking using ¼" (6mm) seams. Clip curves and turn right side out, smoothing seams with fingers. With right sides of cuff pieces together, sew side seams. Repeat for cuff lining. Turn lining right side out and slip

This simple version could be made more ornate with beading, trims, or paint in the embossed areas on either, or both, cuff and stocking. You could also try embossing the velvet yourself by cutting a motif from heavy cardboard, saturating the velvet with spray starch, and, with a hot iron, pressing the fabric facedown over the cutout motif.

inside cuff, right sides together and aligning bottom edges. By hand, baste bottom seam, then machine stitch. Turn cuff right side out, and pin right side of cuff together with wrong side of stocking, matching side seams. By hand, baste top edges together ⅜" (1cm) from edge, then machine stitch.

Turn cuff to outside and finger press seams. For hanger, cut a 1½" × 7" (4 × 18cm) strip of green velvet. Fold long edges to center, then fold strip in half lengthwise, enclosing raw edges. Stitch folded edges together by hand. Fold strip in half and stitch securely in place to inside back edge of stocking top.

Cuff

Pattern shown at 100%

Taffeta Bow Ties Stocking

Who said patchwork had to look countrified? This classic bow-tie pattern rendered in bright colors of silk taffeta makes a truly elegant stocking that will complement the most stylish of holiday decorating schemes.

MATERIALS

½ yd (45.5cm) of iridescent purple silk taffeta

¼ yd (23cm) of iridescent turquoise silk taffeta

Scrap of striped silk dupioni

½ yd (45.5cm) of cotton lining fabric

Small piece of lightweight batting

Matching threads

Nylon monofilament thread

½" (1.5cm) single fold bias tape to match lining

Transfer bow-tie patterns, and stripe direction arrows from page 102 to heavy paper adding ¼" (6mm) seam allowance all around. From striped dupioni fabric cut 6 (A) pieces and 3 (B) pieces having the stripes running in the direction indicated on the pattern piece. From turquoise taffeta, cut 6 (A) pieces. Join the first striped (A) piece to (B) piece, taking care that stripes run perpendicular to each other. Join turquoise (A) piece to striped (A) piece and then to (B) piece. Continue adding (A) pieces, joining them first to the preceding (A) piece, then to (B) piece. Join last (A) piece to (A) pieces on either side, then to (B) piece. Press assembled square flat. Make two more squares in the same manner.

From remaining turquoise taffeta, cut four 4" (10cm) squares, cutting three of the squares in half diagonally. From purple taffeta, cut eight 4" (10cm) squares, cutting one in half diagonally. Assemble strips according to piecing diagram, then sew strips together. Cut two pieces of batting and backing, and one piece of purple taffeta, each 14" × 18" (35.5 x 45.5cm). Lay out one piece of backing face down. Smooth one piece of batting over backing. Lay pieced stocking front, right side up, on top of batting and backing. Baste all layers together. Having machine threaded on top with nylon monofilament, quilt stocking front together along block seam lines and around outside of each bow tie. Mark purple taffeta piece into 3½" (9cm) squares set on the diagonal. Lay remaining backing and batting out same as for front. Lay purple taffeta, marked side up, on top of batting and backing. Pin or baste layers together. Quilt along marked lines, same as for front.

Lay stocking pattern (page 95) on top of quilted front, centering bow ties top to bottom and side to side within pattern outlines. Pin pattern in place and cut out, adding ¼" (6mm) seam allowance on sides and bottom, 1" (2.5cm) on top edge. Flopping pattern piece, pin and cut out stocking back. Using a ¼" (6mm) seam, sew front to back along side and bottom edges. Clip curves and turn right side out, pressing stocking flat. Open out one folded edge of bias tape and turn under ¼" (6mm) at end. Pin to stocking top, having right sides together and raw edges even. Stitch in place. Fold bias tape and top 1" (2.5cm) of stocking to inside. Slipstitch tape in place to inside of stocking. From remaining purple taffeta, cut a strip 2" × 6" (5 × 15cm) for hanger. Fold strip in half lengthwise folding ¼" (6mm) to inside along raw edges. Slipstitch folded edges together. Fold strip in half and sew ends to inside back edge of stocking top.

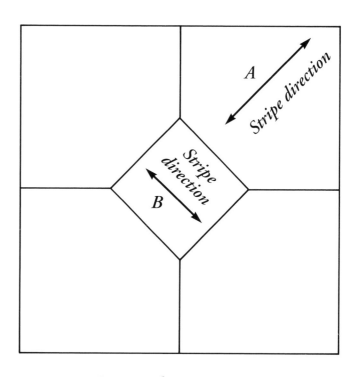

Pattern shown at 100%

~ **VARIATIONS** ~

I used a beautiful stripe for the bow ties shown here, but this would be an excellent place to use those favorite ties from Dad's or your spouse's wardrobe, or the thrift shop. A number of other patchwork patterns would look equally sumptuous when rendered in bright silk taffetas—Log Cabin, Pineapple, and Ocean Waves among them.

Argyle Stocking

This rich red wool stocking is electrified by the addition of the bold plaid of a diamond-shaped appliqué and a border around its upper edge. Bright yellow satin stitching adds an exciting touch.

Enlarge stocking pattern (page 95) and cut two from red wool adding ¼" (6mm) seam allowance all around. Using same pattern, cut two from fusible interfacing and fuse to wrong sides of stocking front and back. From plaid fabric, select motif to be used, fuse adhesive to back and cut out. Place motif in desired position on stocking front and fuse in place. Cut a piece of stabilizer about an inch larger all around than applied motif and pin behind motif area. With machine set on medium width satin stitch and top threaded with contrasting thread, satin stitch around all edges and through motif, following plaid lines. Remove excess stabilizer.

MATERIALS

½ yd (45.5cm) of red wool flannel suiting

¼ yd (23cm) of blue plaid wool

½ yd (45.5cm) of light to midweight fusible interfacing

¼ yd (23cm) tear-away stabilizer

Matching thread

Contrasting thread for satin stitching (pick one of the colors in the plaid)

Fabric glue

Small piece paper backed fusible adhesive

Pin stocking front to back, right sides together, and sew around side and bottom edges using a ¼" (6mm) seam. Clip curves, turn right side out and press seams. From plaid, cut a strip 1¾" × 18" (4.5 × 45.5cm). Using fabric glue, glue strip to right side of top edge of stocking having edges overlap approximately ¼" (6mm), fold one end of strip under ¼" (6mm) and overlap raw end of strip; then trim away any excess strip.

When glue is dry, cut a strip of stabilizer 1" (2.5cm) wide and place behind glued area and satin stitch, same as for front motif, along edge of applied strip. Remove excess stabilizer and fold plaid strip to inside, turning under ¼" (6mm) along raw edge and slip-stictch in place to top of satin stitching. For hanger, cut a strip of plaid 1¼" × 7" (3 × 18cm). Fold in half lengthwise and press. Fold raw edges to center and slipstictch folded edges together. Fold strip in half and sew securely to inside back edge of stocking top.

Floral Felt Stocking

The bold contrast of red against

black in this graphic stocking makes

an undeniably vivid statement hanging

amidst holiday greenery—and it's

very easy to make!

MATERIALS

½ yd (45.5cm) each of red and black felt

1 square of green felt

1 skein of black embroidery floss

Small sharp scissors

Pinking shears

Red and black sewing thread

Fabric glue

Enlarge stocking pattern (page 95), adding 1" (2.5cm) seam allowance on all sides. Cut one stocking piece from red felt. Transfer petal markings and stitching lines (page 108) to felt. Using small sharp scissors, neatly cut out each marked petal. When all petals have been cut out, pin stocking pattern to red felt piece again and cut close to all edges with pinking shears. Pin red stocking to black felt and trim generously around edges to give yourself a manageable piece to work with. Thread needle with six strands of embroidery floss and us-

Petal markings and stitching lines
1 square = 1 inch

Enlarge to 130%

ing a large evenly spaced straight stitch, stitch along marked lines through both layers of felt. When stitching has been completed, leave top edges pinned together; using your sewing machine threaded with red on top and black on bottom, stitch red to black layer along top edge only, beginning and ending ¼" (6mm) inside red edges. Pin assembled piece to another layer of black felt and stitch remaining edges in the same manner. Trim black edges to just beyond the red pinking.

Using leaf pattern, cut eight leaves from green felt and glue in place to stocking front. For hanging loop, cut a 1½" × 6" (4 × 15cm) strip of black felt. Fold long edges to center and stitch in place. Fold strip in half and sew ends securely to inside back edge of stocking top.

∼ VARIATIONS ∼

For a minor change to this design, experiment with different color combinations. Try black or blue over yellow for something more like sunflowers. A slightly rounder petal shape and felt in purples and yellow or white would produce an effect resembling violets or pansies. The centers of the flowers can be embellished with beads, if desired. For an elegant variation on the flower pattern, cut snowflake motifs into blue felt, and layer it over white. Secure the layers with a few swirls stitched with silver thread, adding some snowflake shaped sequins between motifs to make it sparkle.

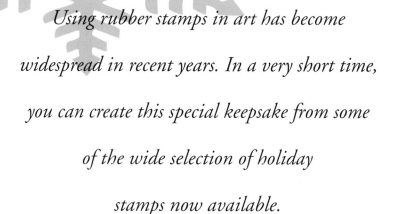

Special Message Stocking

½ yd (45.5cm) of unbleached muslin

1 pkg of red rickrack

Set of alphabet stamps

Assorted rubber stamps with
Christmas motifs

Stamp pad with black fabric ink

Colored pencils

Black fabric marker

Scrap paper

Sewing thread

Note: When stamping on fabric, use a well-inked but not dripping stamp pad. Layer fabric to be stamped onto one or two additional pieces of fabric. I have found that a layer of muslin over a tea towel worked well. Keep edges of stamps clean. You may find it necessary to ink the stamp and then quickly wipe off the edges before stamping to prevent them from showing up on your final work.

Using rubber stamps in art has become widespread in recent years. In a very short time, you can create this special keepsake from some of the wide selection of holiday stamps now available.

Enlarge stocking pattern (page 95), adding ¼" (6mm) seam allowance all around. Trace stocking pattern onto scrap paper and work out placement of stamps. Picture stamps can have a border added with a marker as I have done. Lightly trace stocking shape onto muslin with a pencil. Using paper example (cut it apart and place it on the muslin if it will help), stamp motifs and words onto muslin. Add any additional borders or embellishments desired with marker and pencils.

Cut out stocking front and three additional stocking pieces from plain muslin. Baste center of rickrack along ¼" (6mm) seam line of stocking front. Pin front to back, with right sides together, and sew side and bottom seams, stitching on top of basting. Clip curves and turn right side out. In same manner, stitch rickrack around top edge of stocking.

For lining, pin remaining pieces together and sew sides and bottom using a ⅜" (1cm) seam. Trim seam allowance to ³⁄₁₆" (5mm). Slip lining over stocking, with right sides together, and sew over basting along top edge, leaving an opening at back for turning. Turn lining to inside and slipstitch opening closed. For hanger, cut a 2¼" × 8" (5.5 × 20.5cm) strip of muslin. Fold strip in half lengthwise and sew long edge in a ¼" (6mm) seam. Turn right side out and stitch rickrack along each edge. Fold strip in half and sew ends securely to inside back edge of stocking top.

≈ **VARIATIONS** ≈

This type of stocking would be adorable with a child's letter to Santa worked on the front, perhaps even tracing the child's own handwriting with a marker by using a lightbox or taping the layers to a well-lit window. If you were using a smaller-scale set of letter stamps, you could also work the lettering in a series of patches, applying them to the stocking background, perhaps with a trim sewn over the edges like a frame. Pictures could be added the same way, or a frame could be worked around an image applied directly to the stocking.

See-Through Stocking

The peek-a-boo nature of

this lovely ribbon organza lends a delicate

touch to this stocking but will hide nothing

from inquisitive eyes come

Christmas morning.

MATERIALS

½ yd (45.5cm) of ribbon-striped organza (⅛" [3mm] stripes of satiny-red on a sheer background)

Red velveteen (½ yd [45.5cm] at least; if you purchase 1 yd [91.5cm], you only need to cut one bias strip)

½ yd (45.5cm) of tear-away stabilizer

Small piece of fusible interfacing

Small piece of cardboard, 2" (5cm) wide

30 yds (27.4m) white crochet cotton (I used Cebelia 10)

30 yds (27.4m) opalescent blending filament (I used Balger #32 pearl)

$\mathcal{E}$ nlarge stocking pattern (page 95) onto stabilizer and cuff pattern (page 115) onto paper, adding ¼" (6mm) seam allowance on sides and bottom and ¾" (2cm) hem allowance on top of both. Fold the organza in half, wrong sides together, and using stocking pattern on stabilizer, cut out two stocking pieces, having the stripes running vertically up and down the stocking. Cut two 1½" (4cm) strips of fusible interfacing the width of stocking top. Remove pins from top of stocking pieces and fuse one strip of interfacing to the wrong side of each

stocking piece along the top edge. Pin the organza and the stabilizer stocking layers together again (wrong sides of organza together), and stitch along the seam line around sides and bottom of stocking, beginning and ending ¾" (2cm) below top edge.

Mark bias of velveteen and cut a strip 1¼" (3cm) wide, piecing if necessary. With right side of bias strip facing right side of stocking front and raw edges even, sew bias strip to edge of stocking, beginning and ending ¾" (2cm) from top edge and ending ¾" (2cm) from top on opposite edge. Stretch bias strip slightly along inside curves and push a bit extra through around outside curves to ease the fit; be sure to stitch on top or inside previous stitching. Tear away stabilizer from main body of stocking, leaving the stabilizer in the seam allowance for a little extra body. Fold bias strip to back of stocking, folding under ¼" (6mm) along remaining raw edge. By hand, stitch folded edge to seam line on back of stocking.

Cuff

Pattern shown at 100%

From remaining velveteen, cut four cuff pieces using pattern on page 115. With right sides together, sew (¼" [6mm]) side seams. Turn one cuff piece right side out and place inside remaining cuff. Sew cuff to cuff lining along bottom edge. Clip points and inside corners and turn right side out. Finger press seam flat. With right side of cuff facing wrong side of stocking and top edges aligned, stitch cuff to stocking (leave lining free), using a ⅜" (1cm) seam and easing as necessary to fit. Turn cuff up and fold under ⅝" (1.5cm) on cuff lining. Stitch folded edge to cuff seam, enclosing top edges of cuff and stocking. Fold cuff down to outside. For hanger, cut an 8" (20.5cm) piece of velveteen bias strip and fold both long edges ¼" (6mm) to center. Slipstitch folded edges together. Fold strip in half and sew ends securely to inside back edge of stocking top.

Make eight small tassels as follows: holding crochet cotton and blending filament together, wind strands 30 times around 2" (5cm) piece of cardboard. Then, using a separate piece of crochet cotton slipped between cardboard and wrapped threads, tie a knot tightly around all threads at one edge. Cut all threads at opposite edge of cardboard. Slip knot to inside of threads and using one end of tying thread or additional crochet cotton, wrap tassel tightly eight times about ¼" (6mm) from fold. Fasten off wrapping thread by threading it onto a needle and pulling it under wraps on tassel; clip thread end. Trim ends of tassel, if necessary, and tack a tassel to each point of cuff.

≈ **VARIATIONS** ≈

The ribbon striped organza fabric used here was a somewhat unique type of fabric purchased by mail from Mini-Magic (see Sources, page 126). If you are unable to locate something similar, a beautiful sheer fabric, with some body, could be substituted. Piped and cuffed with a contrasting color fabric, perhaps satin, sheer fabric would look terrific.

Quilted Velvet Stocking

A rich burgundy velveteen is made ornate with the addition of pearls and metallic gold lines quilted diagonally across its face. A line of gold cord around the top edge makes this simply shaped stocking undeniably effective.

MATERIALS

½ yd (45.5cm) of burgundy velveteen

½ yd (45.5cm) of muslin

18" (45.5cm) square piece of lightweight batting

Gold metallic machine embroidery thread

Aapproximately 80 5mm round pearls and 30 pear-shaped pearls

Seam binding

½ yd (45.5cm) of thick gold cord

Ruler

Marking pen

Enlarge stocking pattern (page 95), adding ½" (1.5cm) seam allowance on sides and bottom and 1" (2.5cm) on top. Cut an 18" (45.5cm) square each of burgundy velveteen and muslin. Mark a line on the bias diagonally across the square. Using ruler and marked bias line as beginning point, mark velveteen into a grid of 2" (5cm) squares. Layer marked square right side up on top of batting and muslin, and baste by hand along all marked lines. With machine set on medium-width zigzag stitch and threaded on top with gold metallic thread, satin stitch along

marked lines. Placing pattern on straight grain of fabric (so stitched squares look like diamonds on the stocking), cut out stocking front. Cut stocking back from a single thickness each of velveteen and muslin.

Stitch a pear-shaped pearl close to stitching at top of each diamond and a round pearl to each remaining corner at that intersection. Refrain from sewing pearls to the outer 1½" (4cm) of stocking front until stocking has been assembled. After working the center portion of stocking front, pin it, right sides together, to remaining velveteen piece backed with muslin piece. Sew side and bottom seams, using a ⅜" (1cm) seam. Clip curves and turn stocking right side out. Sew seam binding over top edge, fold hem allowance to inside, and slipstitch binding in place. Finish sewing pearls to stocking front. By hand, sew gold cord around top edge of stocking. For hanger, cut a 2½" × 7" (6.5 × 18cm) strip of velveteen. Fold strip in half lengthwise and sew a ¼" (6mm) seam along long edge. Turn right side out and topstitch along long edges. Fold strip in half and sew ends securely to inside back edge of stocking top.

∾ VARIATIONS ∾

The pattern used here is merely a square turned on point, but a wide variety of patterns could be worked on the velvet background to make a stocking unique to you. You might try a striped effect, incorporating a purchased trim (maybe a lovely brocade ribbon) and working satin stitched scallops down either side with a metallic or other machine embroidery thread. A cuff, embellished or left plain, would be an equally beautiful alternative to the gold cord around the top of this stocking.

Persian Brocade Stocking

½ yd (45.5cm) of brocade fabric

Small piece of black velvet and black lining fabric for cuff

Red tassel, 3" (7.5cm) long

Gold metallic and black sewing machine threads

4" (10cm) square of tear-away stabilizer

12 red pear-shaped, sew-on rhinestones, ¼" (2cm) long

Approximately 120 gold beads, ⁵⁄₃₂" (4mm) in diameter

4 rice-shaped pearl beads, ⁵⁄₁₆" (8mm) long

4½" (11.5cm) of black velvet ribbon, ⅝" (1.5cm) wide

This handsome stocking was inspired by the ornately patterned brocade that makes up its body. Topped with an asymmetrical black velvet cuff, glittering rhinestones, and a bright red tassel, it will add a touch of elegance to your holiday decorations.

Enlarge stocking pattern (page 95) and cuff pattern (page 123), adding a ¼" (6mm) seam allowance on sides and bottom and ½" (1.5cm) on top. Cut two stocking pieces from brocade and one cuff piece each from velvet and lining fabric. With right sides together, sew stocking pieces together along side and bottom using a ¼" (6mm) seam. Clip curves and turn stocking right side out. Press seams flat.

Trace cuff embroidery pattern to tear-away stabilizer, and pin to wrong side of velvet cuff piece centered on the cuff and ⅛" (3mm) above the seam line. With machine set on straight stitch and with a light colored thread in the bobbin (which will act as your guide line on the cuff front), sew along

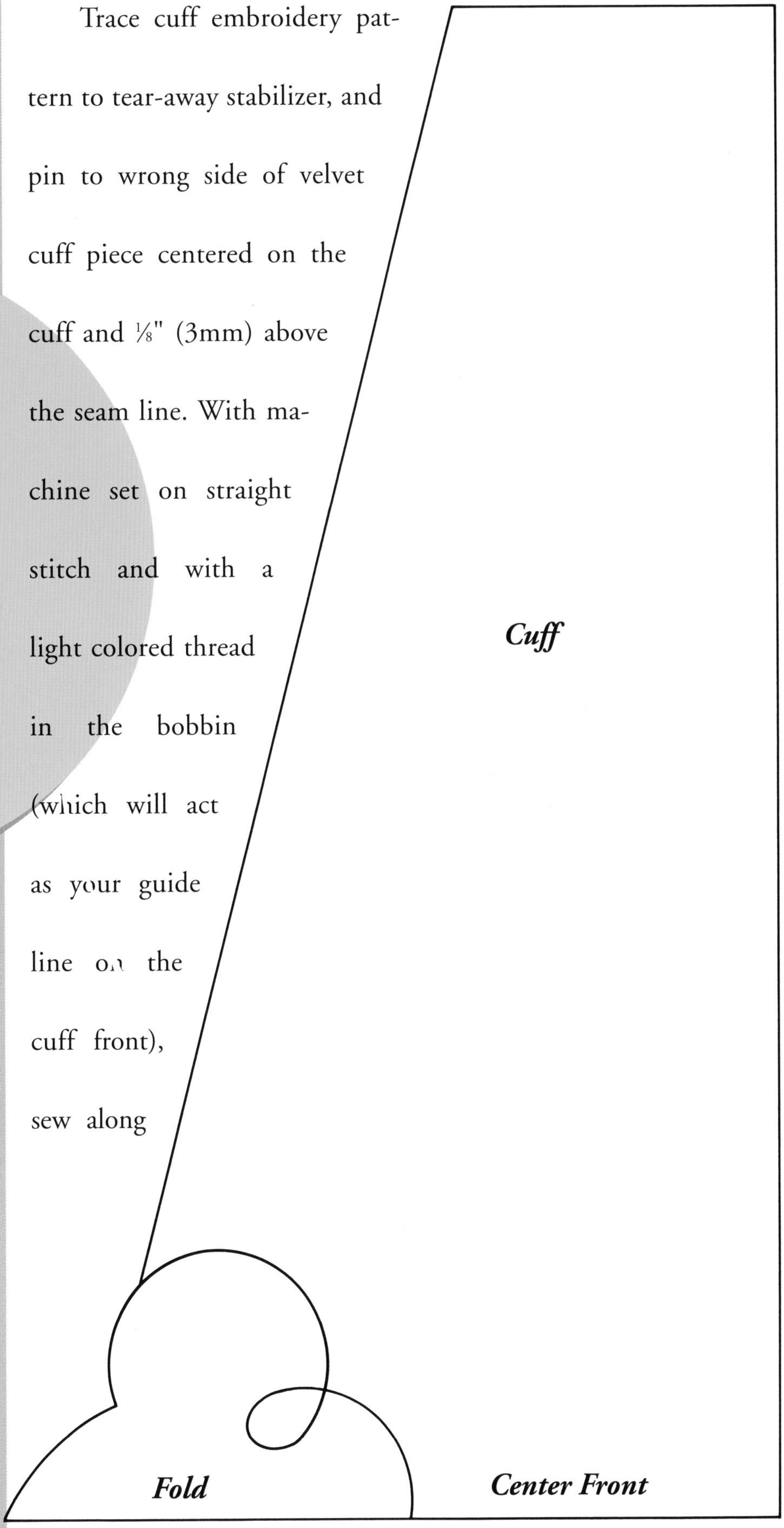

Cuff

Fold

Center Front

Pattern shown at 100%

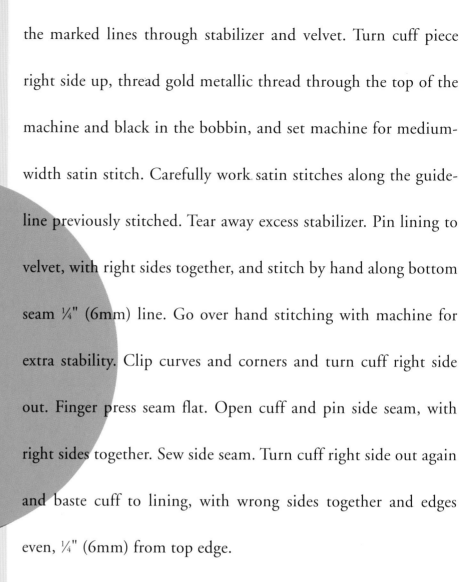

the marked lines through stabilizer and velvet. Turn cuff piece right side up, thread gold metallic thread through the top of the machine and black in the bobbin, and set machine for medium-width satin stitch. Carefully work satin stitches along the guideline previously stitched. Tear away excess stabilizer. Pin lining to velvet, with right sides together, and stitch by hand along bottom seam ¼" (6mm) line. Go over hand stitching with machine for extra stability. Clip curves and corners and turn cuff right side out. Finger press seam flat. Open cuff and pin side seam, with right sides together. Sew side seam. Turn cuff right side out again and baste cuff to lining, with wrong sides together and edges even, ¼" (6mm) from top edge.

To work embellishment of embroidered motif on cuff: stitch one red pear-shaped rhinestone to each side of bottom point inside stitching. Stitch gold beads evenly spaced inside each of three large curved sections as shown, centering a rice-shaped pearl bead inside gold beads on each side section and two in the top section. Along remaining area of cuff, evenly space five red pear-shaped rhinestones from motif to center back and stitch in place. Sew gold beads in arcs below each rhinestone, spacing them as evenly as possible. If desired, hand baste a guideline for gold bead placement with a contrasting color thread.

With right side of cuff facing wrong side of stocking, pin cuff to stocking with top edges even and matching center back seam. Stitch using a ⅜" (1cm) seam. Turn cuff to outside. Tack tassel to cuff lining at center front. Fold velvet ribbon in half and sew securely to inside back edge of stocking top.

∼ VARIATIONS ∼

The design for this stocking was very much driven by the selection of fabrics available in my local stores. An alternate selection of brocade may suggest a different theme to you. Instead of Persian, you might find something with an Oriental or South American feel. You can then alter the cuff and/or trim to be more reflective of that culture. Inspiration for embellishment can be found in decorative sourcebooks in your local bookseller's or library's art section.

Sources

❖ ❖ ❖ ❖ ❖

Most items used to create the projects in this book are readily available at crafts stores around the country. Here is a list of reputable mail-order suppliers with whom I have dealt.

Enterprise Art
P.O. Box 2918
Largo, FL 34649
(813) 536-1492

Stocks a large variety of beads and jewelry findings, including conchos.

Keepsake Quilting
Route 25B
P.O. Box 1618
Centre Harbor, NH 03226-1618
(800) 525-8086

Stocks a wide variety of cotton fabrics for crafting and quilting, including ¼-yard (23cm) collections of plaids and 1930s-style fabrics, as well as other themed fabric, battings, quilting patterns, and accessories.

Mini-Magic
3910 Patricia Drive
Columbus, OH 43220
(614) 457-3687

Stocks an incredible variety of fabrics, chiffons, taffetas, silks, and velvets, as well as ribbons and laces.

Nancy's Notions
333 Beichl Avenue
P.O. Box 683
Beaver Dam, WI 53916-0683
(800) 833-0690

Stocks decorative threads and sewing supplies, as well as a nice selection of synthetic suede, including animal prints, fusible adhesives, and battings.

Newark Dressmaker Supply
6473 Ruch Road
P.O. Box 20730
Lehigh Valley, PA 18002-0730
(610) 837-7500

Stocks sewing notions and some beads, pearls, and other trims.

Index

❖ ❖ ❖ ❖ ❖